FORCES '87

FORCES '87

Marshall Cavendish

Published by
Marshall Cavendish House
58 Old Compton Street,
London W1V 5PA

Edited and designed by
DPM Services Ltd
19 Short's Gardens
London WC2H 9AT

Editor	Mark Dartford
Art Editor	Graham Beehag
Editorial Consultant	Geoffrey Cornish
Production Controller	Steve Roberts
Picture Research	John Moore/MARS

© Marshall Cavendish Limited
MCMLXXXVI
ISBN 0 86307 637 8

Typeset by Bookworm Typesetting, Manchester.
Printed and bound by Dai Nippon Printing Co., Hong Kong

CONTENTS

British soldiers of the UN peacekeeping force in Cyprus.

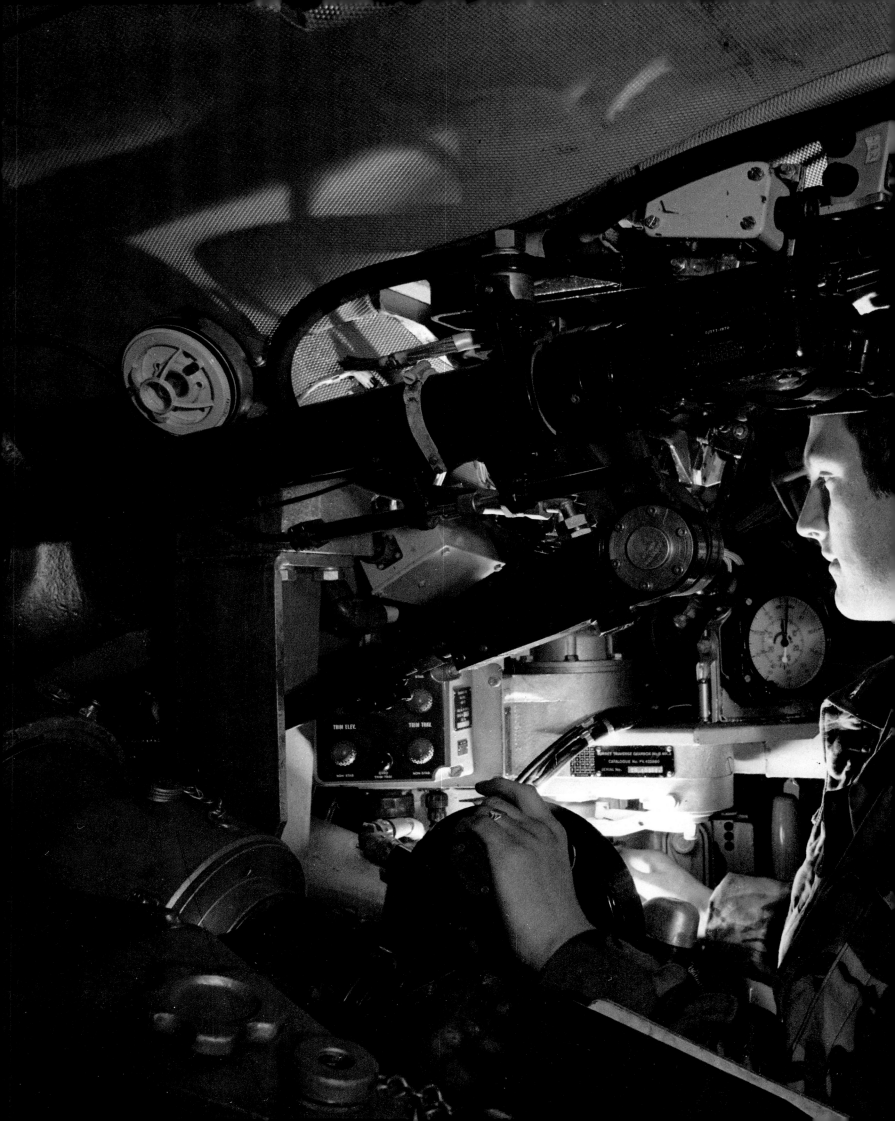

INTRODUCTION

In the year since publication of Forces '86, the tide of events both political and military concerning defence planning and establishment has gathered momentum. Secretary of State Michael Heseltine resigned following disagreement with Cabinet colleagues over the Westland Helicopters affair. On the Falkland front, tentative reconciliatory talks between British MPs and Argentinian ministers have begun – though the question of sovereignty over the islands remains firmly *off* the table. Meanwhile further cuts in the Forces conventional budget have forced defence planners to examine cheaper ways of maintaining credible manning levels. Forces '87 looks at the wider implications of these matters with chapters on the South Atlantic, the world of the multi-national warplane business and the increasingly important role of the Nation's committed part-time soldiers – as well as reviewing recent NATO exercises, the role of the Navy's minesweeping fleet and taking a glimpse at the bewildering world of modern military technology.

Interior of a Chieftan tank.

Chapter 1

SOUTH ATLANTIC: BEYOND THE FALKLANDS

With the Mount Pleasant airport now open, and the island garrison at full strength, the 'Kelpers' are beginning to adapt to the new way of life these changes have brought. Meanwhile, the global and strategic importance of the Falkland islands in terms of defence and natural resources has continued to grow.

Large scale construction work is having an effect on the way of life in the Falklands.

The most important event in the Falklands in 1985 was the opening of the 8,500 foot long main runway of the new Mount Pleasant airport. The islands were thereby restored to the highways of international communication for the first time since the Yankee whalers gave up calling at Port Stanley on their way to the rich hunting grounds of the South Atlantic. It was the lack of such an airfield with a sufficiently long runway to take front line aircraft which enabled the Argentinians to occupy the Falklands with such ease four years ago. The most potent aircraft on Stanley's tiny airfield was a light plane belonging to the Governor, Rex Hunt, a former Spitfire pilot.

The flying boot was, of course, on the other foot when the Argentinians came under attack from the British task force. Although they were able to fly their counter insurgency Pucaras from the island's airstrips, their Skyhawks, Daggers and Super Etendards had to operate at extreme range from their bases on the mainland and with fuel running out could afford to spend only a few minutes over their targets. As it was a number of them had to ditch on the way home.

Now Britain has a potent base on the Falklands. The Harriers which provided the "thin blue line" during the fighting have been replaced by Phantoms which will themselves be reinforced by modern Tornados if trouble threatens. The proven Nimrod maritime reconnaissance aircraft will watch for signs of naval activity and, if necessary, call up Buccaneers to strike at any Argentinian ships bound for the islands. Moreover, at the first sign of trouble, reinforcing troops can now be flown in by TriStars and VC 10s with little more than 36 hours notice.

Cost of peace

It has cost a great deal of money. The lastest figures show that some £430 million has been spent on the Mount Pleasant project. How tantalising then, to reflect that successive British governments refused to spend a mere £4 million to extend the runway at Stanley before the events of 1982. And that a few strike aircraft would probably have been sufficient to dissuade General Galtieri and his junta from their adventure. This does not detract from the tremendous achievement of the men who have built the project and seem to have got little praise for their efforts. To construct the new runway they moved eight million tons of rock and soil, often under appalling weather conditions. And they did it in just twelve months. Engineering plant worth £25 million had to be unloaded and a merchant ship was secured to the East Cove by Bailey bridge so that the equipment could be got ashore. Thirty thousand tons of material went across that bridge every month.

Maurice Chamming, regional director of the Property Services Agency, told Robert Fox of the BBC – who was awarded the MBE for his coverage of the fighting – that "We have the equivalent of three army battalions of men here. All of them are away from home with nothing

Above: Mr. Gordon Jewkes who in October 1985 replaced Sir Rex Hunt as Governor of the Falkland Islands, in Government House, Stanley, shortly after his arrival.

like military discipline behind them and nowhere to go but the site.

"It is amazing that we have had so little trouble and got so much willing work out of them. Some days in the winter they worked on in blinding snow with the wind bringing the chill factor down to minus thirty degrees."

Completion of the airfield and its capacity for rapid reinforcement means that the garrison can be allowed to shrink to just over 2000 men and the government has been able to forecast a drastic decrease in the amount of money the Falklands are costing the British taxpayer.

The Treasury reckoned that the defence of the islands would cost £288,000 for each islander in 1985, £234,000 in 1986 and £156,000 in 1987. With the tailing off of military construction and the shrinkage of the garrison total expenditure is expected to fall from £552 million in 1986 to £192 million in 1988-89. However, the balance of economy against effectiveness must be maintained for if the garrison was allowed to shrink to such a

low level that the Argentinians were able to capture the airport by a coup de main, it would be impossible for any future task force to recapture the Islands.

Major-General Peter de la Billiere, Military Commissioner of the Falklands, who as an SAS officer has won more medals for gallantry in "peacetime" than any other soldier, spelt out his determination that this would never happen: "We're here to make sure that what happened in 1982 never happens again and to ensure that the democracy we won back through the sacrifice of British lives is not given away again through inadequate force levels."

Shift to air power

He has now moved on to another job and his replacement exemplifies the swing of emphasis from army operations on the islands to air power, from the yomping Marines and the extraordinary exploits of the SAS and the SBS to the brute power of the jet engine. The new military boss is an RAF officer, Air Commodore R.J. "Kip" Kemball.

To highlight the change to what is regarded as normalcy the post of Military Commissioner has been dropped and Kemball has assumed the traditional title of Commander British Forces, Falkland Islands. The other immediate effect of the opening of Mount Pleasant to modern long range aircraft is of course that the "Kelpers" are no longer dependent on the Argenti-

Left: An Army Chinook helicopter delivering another unit to the Portacabin camp. Below: Dumper trucks carrying construction materials during building of the new airport at Mount Pleasant. The base operates both conventional fighters and troop-carrying passenger aircraft to enable rapid reinforcement in emergency.

Above: Conventional 'Oberon' class submarine in Stanley harbour, ideally suited to the shallow waters surrounding the Falkland Islands. The military presence is seen by Moscow as a strategic operation.

nians, as they were before 1982, for their aerial connections. While they are delighted by this, their joy is not unalloyed.

In the first place the Ministry of Defence intends to retain sole use of the airport until the entire project including a second runway of 5,000 feet is completed. Secondly the journey out to Mount Pleasant is no easy matter, involving an aerial hop of thirty miles, the facilities are primitive and the cost of a return flight to London is £1,900, although islanders are entitled to concessionary fares which bring the cost down to £1,050.

No doubt these irritations will be smoothed out in time but at the moment they and the immediate use of the new airfield as the main bastion of Fortress Falklands tend to obscure the more important long-term impact of Mount Pleasant and its capabilities on the South Atlantic and the development of the Antarctic. The Soviet Union has already begun to complain that Great Britain, with American backing, is building a NATO nuclear base in the Falklands designed to control the Southern Atlantic. Moscow projects the Falklands conflict not as a quarrel between two previously friendly nations over a miniscule piece of real estate, but as part of the world-wide clash between Communism and Capitalism.

There is some logic to their argument for Mount Pleasant will now give the west a base from which its long-range maritime reconnaissance and anti-submarine warfare aircraft can scour the South Atlantic. The importance of such a base has been recognised by strategists ever since the abrogation of the Simonstown Naval Agreement by the Harold Wilson government in 1974.

This severance of naval cooperation between Great Britain and South Africa allied to the embargo on the supply of military material to that country because of its apartheid policies has led to the withering away of the South African navy. Its two most powerful surface ships – themselves only frigates – are in reserve and the navy concentrates on coastal work to prevent the seaborne infiltration of saboteurs and terrorists. And when the South African Air Force's venerable Shackletons were retired last November South Africa no longer had any credibility as "Guardian of the Cape Sea Route."

South Atlantic Alliance

At one time there was much talk of a SATO to work alongside NATO. The idea was that South Africa, with Britain, the United States and friendly South American States like Argentina, Chile and Brazil would form a South Atlantic Treaty Organisation to guard against Russian expansion in the South Atlantic.

The demise of South Africa as a naval power and the continuing quarrel between Britain and Argentina has ended such talk. But the need for such a protective agreement has never been greater. It was the late Leonid Brezhnev who, in 1973, said: "It is our aim to gain control of the great treasure houses of the modern world, the energy treasure house of the Middle East and the mineral treasure house of Southern Africa."

Although Brezhnev is dead that particular aim remains in the forefront of his successor's thinking. Apart from the minerals, 60% of Europe's and 20% of America's oil imports and 25% of Europe's food imports pass round the Cape of Good Hope. And the only viable force that South Africa has to protect its sealanes are three small Daphne class submarines.

At the same time the Russian navy has established itself in Angola where it keeps an 8,500 ton capacity floating drydock. This drydock, based at Luanda, can handle most of the major Russian fighting ships. There is an average presence of six to eight Russian naval vessels off the West African coast while Tupolev 95 Bear D maritime reconnaissance aircraft deploy to Luanda in pairs about three or four times a year. It is also known that Soviet submarines make regular patrols in the South Atlantic but information is sketchy simply because without the South African Shackletons, nobody is keeping watch on the vast open spaces of the South Atlantic.

It seems that Western shipping in any major crisis would be left undefended from Soviet attacks while Russian shipping would be well protected by Soviet naval vessels and aircraft operating from their bases in Southern and Western Africa. Given Brezhnev's threat to the "mineral treasure house of Southern Africa," the importance of the strategic trade routes round both Capes and the experience of the damage caused by German raiders during both World Wars, it is extraordinary that the West should pay such little attention to such a vital area.

In these circumstances it is natural for Moscow to look on Mount Pleasant in terms of the global struggle. The men in the Kremlin are not concerned about a picayune quarrel between Britain and Argentina – except when they can use it to their own political advantage – but they are concerned about a modern airfield which could have a strategic effect on an area which was fast becoming a Russian lake. And if anyone should think that there are no electronic spyships among the fleet of Russian trawlers fishing off the Falklands, they are doubtless very much mistaken.

The implications of Mount Pleasant are not lost on NATO's planners. Removed from the embarrassment of having to rely on the apartheid government of South Africa and less than stable allies in South America it may well be that NATO will see the airfield and Fortress Falkland as the lynchpin on which it could build a strategy for the South Atlantic. Certainly there has never been any demarcation line which, as Admiral Harry Train, NATO's Supreme Allied Commander, Atlantic, has pointed out, would "prevent collective planning, manoeuvres or operations south of the Tropic of Cancer."

Antarctic factor

So we now have two assured roles for Mount Pleasant: 1. The connecting of the Falklands to the rest of the world. 2. Their defence against any future attack from Argentina. We also have a perceived role: that of NATO base in the South Atlantic. And then there is the long term possible role with the Falklands as the forward base for the exploitation of the Antarctic.

The fact is that nobody knows what is going to happen in the Antarctic. It is believed that there are vast mineral and hydrocarbon deposits beneath the ice. Just how much, is not known.

What is known is that the commercial exploitation of these deposits will be horribly difficult – men will be working in the world's most unforgiving climate – and desperately expensive. There is no chance of any commercial work being undertaken there this century. But countries with claims on Antarctica are already jostling for position. The Argentinians have even gone to the extent of flying pregnant women there so that their children can claim to be citizens of Antarctica by birth.

The situation is presently controlled by the "Consultative Parties" which are those states that had an active presence in Antarctica during the International Geophysical Year (1957-1958) and signed the Antarctic Treaty in 1959. Other states qualified later by conduct-

Above: Supplies and equipment coming ashore at East Cove, the port for the Mount Pleasant airport construction site. With the increasing loss of stabiliy in South Africa, the facility is of growing importance to NATO.

ing "substantial scientific research there, such as the establishment of a scientific station or despatch of a scientific expedition". The treaty guarantees the territory's exclusive use for peaceful purposes and prohibits any activities of a military nature, nuclear explosions and the storage or disposal of radioactive material. And, if there is any suspicion that anybody is breaking the

Above left: Rapier SAM anti-aircraft missile system, with attendant operative. Below left: Members of a British antarctic survey team setting up an automatic weather station (AWS) on an island in the Bigourdan Fjord, in the Antarctic Peninsular. The AWS is an unmanned weather station, running on batteries.
Above: Scientists from China's antarctic expedition pose with theodolite and parasol. When bored, their members took to stoning the region's many penguins, which did not endear them to other members of the antarctic community.

rules of the Antarctic club an inspection systems allows any "Consultative Party" to examine the Antarctic facilities of the others.

The 12 original "Consultative Parties" – Argentina, Australia, Belgium, Chile, France, Japan, New Zealand, Norway, South Africa, the Soviet Union, the United Kingdom and the United States have since been joined by Poland, West Germany, India and Brazil. Belgium and Norway no longer maintain permanent stations.

The Chinese sent out ther first expedition in November 1984 but they blotted their copy-book. Their bored workmen took to stoning the penguins and at one stage they were in danger of being drummed out of the Antarctic club. The Australians have also been in trouble for allowing tons of rubbish to accumulate round their two camps.

This may all seem nicely cosy but the Treaty has performed one great service: it has frozen the various territorial claims in the region "for the indefinite duration of the Treaty." Seven of the original members, Argentina,

Australia, Chile, France, New Zealand, Norway and the United Kingdom have made claims with Australia, New Zealand and Great Britain claiming three quarters of the Antarctic between them. None of these claims have been recognised by the other parties and danger lay in the fact that the British, Argentinian and Chilean claims overlapped. They still do because the treaty, while refusing to recognise any state's territorial sovereignty in the region, protects the legal rights of those signatories who claim sovereignty. At the same time it does not allow new claims to be put forward during the Treaty's lifetime.

An "elegant arrangement"

Described in diplomatic terms as "an elegant arrangement", the Treaty has worked well. But strains are beginning to show. The Treaty failed to cover the question of mineral resources and with the possibility of such resources being found the "Consultative Parties" have been trying to stitch together a mineral resource regime within the Treaty.

At the same time it has come under attack from outside by those nations, mainly Third World countries too poor to send out scientific expeditions, who fear that they will be cheated out of the taking part in what they believe will be the world's last great gold rush and they are demanding United Nations control of the Antarctic. Mrs Thatcher's view of the situation is that "If the Antarctic were brought under the control of a world-

Above: Russian trawlers and factory ships are among the fishing fleets of many nations currently netting rich profits from the seas around the islands. Despite pressure from the islanders, the British Government has so far failed to impose a 200 mile fishing zone in the area for the simple reason that it could not be effectively policed if introduced. The islanders have never been serious fishermen.
Right: Wired up, zipped up penguin off for a day's research. This penguin carries a pack which will enable its movements to be followed over several days, as part of an antarctic research project.

wide agency, possibly within the UN, it would be far more difficult to achieve the level of cooperation that has been possible within the Antarctic Treaty framework. Because of the sovereignty complication and the possible extension of the common heritage concept to resources, an Antarctic Authority could prove even harder to set up than a Sea-Bed Authority. And ill-functioning international arrangement might tempt countries active in the Antarctic to act unilaterally with possible risks for the environment and with damaging effects for Antarctic scientific cooperation.

"The vast investments required to exploit Antarctic resources would be made in the medium term only if clear cut and stable regimes were seen to be operating. Whatever new arrangements are made, the fact remains that the real problems of exploiting Antarctica's resources are practical rather then legal. It is not the restrictive nature of the Antarctic Treaty so much as the physical restrictions of the Antarctic environment that have made it possible for only a small group of nations to undertake exploration and research in the area."

All this may well be a rush after fool's gold. Lord Shackleton in his Report said: "While there is a reasonable probability that hydrocarbons exist in certain areas of Antarctica . . . there is insufficient evidence to make an overall prognostication over the mineral resources of the Continent."

Lord Shackleton returned to this theme in an article last year in which he wrote: "Although of immense scientific importance, the Antarctic is at present of little economic value and its mineral and other resources (fisheries apart) are unlikely to be exploited in this century."

However, he went on to say that "It would be absurd to conclude that they could not at some time be of value and therefore a source of temptation. While I have always favoured some form of international ownership or administration of the Antarctic, the fact is that if Britain were to give up the Falklands the British position and influence and that of the British Antarctic Survey would be gravely weakened. This could lead to the pursuit of purely national interests and even of conflict. The maintenance of British rights in the Falklands and South Georgia is a key to future peace in the whole region . . ."

Farewell speech

Sir Rex Hunt, knighted after the recapture of the Falklands, was even more blunt. In his farewell speech as Civil Commissioner in October 1985, he said: "Any British government of whatever colour that gives up any bit of real estate in the South Atlantic for the next fifty years, until we know what is exploitable in the South Atlantic, will be blamed, and rightfully, by future British generations for being irresponsible and short-sighted."

Thus we come back to the notion of the Falklands not only as a powerful bastion against possible Argentinian attack and as a base to protect the South Atlantic from the Communists but also as Britain's advance depot for the exploitation of the Antarctic in the 21st Century.

Meanwhile, back on the islands, the "Kelpers" were dealing with more mundane affairs. Like how to persuade the British government to impose a 200 mile fishing zone round the island to conserve their stocks of fish – mainly hake and blue whiting – and to earn an estimated £10 million a year from licenses sold to the trawlers from Spain, Japan, Taiwan and the Eastern bloc which are reaping a rich harvest from the seas around the Falklands.

Some 50 Polish, Spanish and Taiwanese trawlers have obtained permission, but not licenses, to fish inside the 150 mile "Protection Zone" and last year the

Poles paid nearly £500,000 in harbour dues and customs. But a further 50 trawlers from Japan and the Eastern Bloc do not officially fish within the Protection Zone and only call into Port Stanley when they need urgent medical treatment for crew-members. The islanders argue that they are depleting the fish stocks without paying for them. Whitehall, however, is reluctant to impose a 200 mile fishing zone for the simple reason that it does not have enough ships to police such a zone. The Royal Navy can barely sustain its present commitments.

Among the ships patrolling the Protection Zone is the Royal Fleet Auxiliary vessel, Reliant, a former container ship of 27,867 tons which has been converted under the "Arapaho" scheme into a helicopter support vessel.

It sailed some 75,000 miles around the Falklands in 1985, flying five Sea King helicopters off its huge deck. It is described as a cost-effective method of providing Anti Submarine Warfare cover to the Falklands but it remains an expedient, something known in the Royal Navy as a "lash-up". The point is that if the navy has to use such a ship for ASW, where is it going to find the frigates needed to maintain a fully protected fishing zone?

Argentinian involvement in fisheries

What the British government would like to see would be a multilateral fisheries regime organised by the United Nations Food and Agricultural Organisation which would be run with the cooperation of the Argentinians. Not suprisingly, despite the mutual economic and conservationist benefits that would undoubtedly stem from such an agreement, the Argentinians are not keen on this idea. For they fear that to do so would imply recognition of Britain's right to the islands. And that they will never do. What they have done is to agree to an FAO research programme into the region's fish stocks.

So, while the foreign trawlers make off with huge catches of fish whose depleted stocks are, according to an investigation carried out by a British expert, causing concern but are not critical, the islanders fume over their lost revenue and the British government finds itself powerless to take effective action.

Other developments on the islands are progressing more favourably if still extremely slowly. About 400,000 acres, mostly foreign-owned, have been subdivided. There are now 28 small farms each owned by an islander who, in most cases, is a former employee of the four big ranches which have been sub-divided. Output on these new farms has been increased by 15%.

Experiments have been made with exporting crabmeat. A woollen mill has been established to produce Falkland sweaters from local wool. There is a new dairy and a slaughter-house which meets EEC standards. Gradually things are beginning to happen. But it is all taking so long. The Falkland Islands Development Corporation and the Overseas Development Agency have been called "funereal and sluggish", a description disputed by Mr Simon Armstrong, General Manager of the

Above: Richard Cockwell and his wife of Fox Bay East who have founded the Falkland Islands first woollen mill. Wool and mutton remain the Islands chief resource. The mill will produce Falkland Island sweaters for export.

FIDC, who says: "We are no longer a ghost organisation. We have become a real corporation doing real things with real money."

One aspect of development which has been widely canvassed but in which little has taken place is tourism. Although brochures have been prepared, the high cost of the projected air fares and, especially, the lack of accommodation has prevented any effective steps being taken. No decision will be taken on the future of tourism in the Falklands until the second runway is completed.

The FIDC has, however, plans to build a chain of prefabricated mini-hotels on some of the islands which are particularly rich in wildlife. But here, they come up against one of the Catch 22 problems of the islands: there are not enough houses to attract the skilled craftsmen to the islands in order to build more houses. To get round this problem the FIDC is shipping out 54 prefabricated timber houses along with the skilled labour to erect them.

This leads on to another problem: the only viable ways of developing the islands seem to involve flooding them with newcomers which is hardly what the "Kelpers" envisaged during the fight for Port Stanley. (The population is now 1,800, a growth of 4% since 1982.)

And never in their wildest dreams during the sound and fury of the fighting did they think they would become the subject of criticism from conservationist groups who fear that the development of their islands will not only have a harmful effect on the Falklands sea-mammal and bird population but will reach into the Antarctic itself.

Greenpeace sail onto the scene

Greenpeace has already made one expedition into the Antarctic ice in its attempts to make the Polar Continent a national park and has expressed its fear that the new airfield will encourage commercial companies to use the Falklands as a base for exploitation of the region.

The islanders recognise, perhaps better than anyone else, that they will never be able to go back to their old, quiet, neglected way of life. They have become the symbols of too many fears, of too much politicking, and they have been the cause of too much spilt blood and spent money for that to happen.

Above: FIPASS floating dock installation in Stanley harbour. The installation, which includes dock facility, floating crane and warehousing, enables supplies to be brought ashore for the army garrison on the island. The existing docks in Port Stanley were insufficiently equipped.

Top left: Beer being unloaded from a warehouse holding army supplies in Port Stanley. The celebrated Penguin Ale (top right) went out of business, so drink has now to be imported from the UK. **Left:** The Islands do not afford much opportunities for relaxation for the soldiers garrisoned there, but for hardy windsurfers there is plenty of water and plenty of wind. **Below:** The new Portacabin facilities are comfortable, warm, and fully serviced.

Above left: An army ordnance officer stands by piles of various types of Argentinian ammunition discovered since the war, and now due for demolition. Below left: Track cleared through Argentine minefield, to allow the laying of a fuel pipeline. Above: A lingering relic of the war. One of the many warning signs left up around uncleared Argentinian minefields. The army has given up trying to find a way of removing the thousands of minimum-metal mines laid during the occupation.

The continued presence of a garrison, even though drastically reduced, means that except in the remotest parts of "the camp" they are reminded daily of what has happened and what they have become. The soldiers really don't like being there. It is a five-month posting away from their wives and families and there is not enough "local talent" for the young men. Another constant reminder that life will never be the same again are the signposts painted with bright red skull and crossbones marking the still uncleared Argentinian minefields. Despite three years of work by the Royal Engineers more than 15,000 anti-personnel mines are still in position. There are 111 minefields fenced off around Port Stanley and another 30 out in the country. Most of these minefields remain unmapped because the Argentinian army did not keep proper records. They also remain mostly undetectible because the mines are made of plastic. The Sappers, despite using the most sophisticated techniques – including sideways scanning radar – have suffered a number of serious casualties and have been forced to halt their mine-clearing operation until some new method is evolved which will enable them to pinpoint the individual mines.

Little trouble but some drunkenness

The islanders have also been effected by the presence of some 2,000 workmen. It may well be, as Mr Chamming claims, that there has been surprisingly little trouble but there has been drunkenness – not that sobriety

is a particular virtue in the Falklands – along with fights and stabbings.

The soldiers and workmen have also brought a different way of life to the islands, with discos and squash courts and videos. There is, moreover, a suggestion of even more drastic change in the future for the American company, Firsland Oil and Gas, has been granted the islands' first oil prospecting licence. It confirmed its long term commitment by buying 220 square mile Douglas Station which covers some 12½% of East Falkland and during its first year of life it has carried out a series of geological studies.

The Falklanders are, however, prepared to accept these upheavals as long as they can be assured that they will remain British and the Falklands and will not become Argentinian and the Malvinas. And about that, they have the gravest of suspicions. Most of them are convinced that sooner or later they will be "sold down the river" and that when Mrs Thatcher ceases to be Prime Minister it will be sooner rather than later.

Mr Gordon Jewkes, their new Governor – the old post was restored on Sir Rex Hunt's retirement – has done his best to reassure them. The former Consul General in Chicago, who with his love of hiking should fit in well, told the islanders that his appointment signalled no change in policy. He insisted that while he was in favour of talks to normalise commercial relations with Argentina, "unless they are prepared to come to the table and not raise the question of sovereignty, I don't think we are going to get very far."

The British government reinforced Mr Jewkes' stand by stating that while it was seeking better relations with a democratic Argentina, "we are not prepared to resume discussion of the future of the Islands with the Argentine government. The question of sovereignty must be set aside."

That was sweet music to the "Kelpers" but they could take small comfort from events outside their own protected zone. Throughout 1985 the row over the sinking of the Belgrano kept sputtering into flame. Clive Ponting, the civil servant who leaked secret documents to Labour M.P. Tam Dalyell, the relentless pursuer of Mrs Thatcher over the Belgrano, was tried under the Official Secrets Act and to the surprise of many was found not guilty by the jury.

Dalyell warned by Court

Perhaps the only consolation Mrs Thatcher and the Falklanders got from the trial was the warning issued to Mr Dalyell by Mr Justice McCowan about his comments while the trial was going on: "If you cannot control yourself even after this warning, I may be driven to put you somewhere where you cannot comment."

The acquittal of Mr Ponting was followed by a report from the Commons Select Committee on Foreign Affairs which had been inquiring into the Belgrano affair. Demonstrating the deep political divisions surrounding the affair, the committee split on party lines. The

Tories accepted Mrs Thatcher's version of the circumstances leading to the sinking of the Argentinian cruiser while the Labour members made it clear – in Parliamentary language – that they thought she was lying.

The three leaders in opposition, Mr Neil Kinnock, Mr David Steel and Dr David Owen, are united in their opposition to what they believe is Mrs Thatcher's intransigence over the Falklands. Dr Owen spelt out his fears predicting that Britain's unyielding attitude could lead to serious tensions in its relations with the United States and Europe.

In July, there was the first sign of an easing in Britain's position with the lifting of the trade embargo on Argentina. It came exactly a year after the tentative Anglo-Argentinian talks in Berne collapsed on the grounds that the Argentines were insisting on discussing the question of sovereignty.

However, the olive twig was brushed aside by the Argentinians who replied with an offer to resume negotiations to restore normal relations which in turn was rejected by Foreign Minister Sir Geoffrey Howe because, "sovereignty was not up for discussion."

The Argentinians then leaked the guarantees they were prepared to give the Falklanders in return for sovereignty. They included dual citizenship, local autonomy, their own currency, English as an official language and a treaty covering these proposals guaranteed by three members of the United Nations. They also suggested that there should be a 10 year period of joint administration leading up to the incorporation of the Falklands as a separate province of Argentina.

While all this was going on President Raul Alfonsin, the democratically elected President of Argentina who replaced the military junta, was conducting a skilful international "hearts and minds" campaign.

He put the disgraced generals on trial, thus marking his abhorrence of their policies, and announced his intentions of getting the Malvinas back by peaceful means. He met Neil Kinnock in Paris in September and two weeks later he met David Steel in Madrid. After the Madrid meeting, the Argentinian President and the Liberal leader issued a joint communique calling for pre-

Below: Argentine President Alfonsin and Liberal Party Leader David Steel shake hands after their private meeting in Madrid in autumn 1985.

parations for negotiations on the future of the Falklands to begin without delay. The talks, they said, should include the question of sovereignty.

Argentina takes advantage

The Falklanders read about this with horror. It confirmed all their worst fears about the future if Mrs Thatcher should happen to be defeated at the next election. The Argentinians, naturally enough, regarded it as a great coup and they pushed home their propaganda advantage.

President Alfonsin, interviewed on BBC's Newsnight, said "I'd very much like to talk to Mrs Thatcher." And Danta Caputo, his Foreign Minister, in another interview, said "I would really love to have a public debate with British representatives on this so that our position can be known to the British public."

They were setting the scene for the United Nations debate on the Falklands in late November. The debate

Below: Bristow Sikorsky S61 Helicopter together with an army Lynx in flight over the Camp. Helicopters remain the most practical form of transport over this rugged terrain.

ended in two heavy defeats for Great Britain and left behind the feeling that its representatives had overplayed their hand. The Assembly did not take kindly to an attempt by Sir John Thomson to insert an amendment reaffirming the Falkland Islanders' right to self-determination. Members felt that self-determination did not apply in the case of the Falklands. Having refused the amendment, the Assembly then voted on the resolution which had been drafted by the Argentine and sponsored by a group of non-aligned states.

The motion, carefully avoiding the use of the emotive word, sovereignty, requested the British and Argentine governments "to initiate negotiations with a view to finding the means to resolve peacefully and definitively the problem pending between both countries, including all aspects of the future of the Falkland Islands." It was passed by the overwhelming majority of 107 to 4 with 41 abstentions.

What was significant was that only Oman, Belize and the Solomon Islands voted with Britain while her Common Market partners France, Greece, Italy and Spain voted against her, as did the Commonwealth countries, Australia and Canada and her great ally, the United

Above: Search and rescue helicopter at Navy Point, near Port Stanley. Note ground crews temporary accommodation structure in the background. Below: An islander reads the inscription and roll of honour on the memorial to 2 Para on the site of their battle for Goose Green during Operation Corporate.

States. The American vote was particularly telling because during the fighting in 1982, the United States backed Britain in every way. The vote was greeted with jubilation in Buenos Aires. Banner headlines proclaimed: "An overwhelming victory for Argentina." And the conservative La Nacion said the vote showed how Britain's "extreme intransigence can end up alienating even the closest allies."

In the House of Commons, Mrs Thatcher once again came under attack with Dr Owen arguing that: "Negotiation does not mean surrender. It is perfectly possible to enter negotiations on all aspects while reserving our position on sovereignty."

Mr Kinnock said the vote demonstrated dwindling support for the policy of the government and its isolation in an area where it would need all the alliances it could get. And the all-party South Atlantic Council which is chaired by the Tory MP, Mr Cyril Townsend,

said Britain should have voted for the resolution rather than against it, for "sooner or later the British Government will have to respond positively and attempt to negotiate a peaceful settlement acceptable to us, to the Argentinians and to the Islanders."

Mrs Thatcher did not attempt to conceal her displeasure at being let down by her allies at the United Nations and she replied to her critics in characteristic style: "Anyone who thinks that a motion that contains the phrase 'negotiations on all aspects of the future of the Falklands' does not contain sovereignty must be absolutely bonkers."

None of this gave the Falklanders any reassurance whatsoever. Despite the cheerful presence of the garrison, the confident rumble from the Phantoms as they roar off on patrol down their new runway, the reassuring sight of the "grey funnel line" ships and the promise of better economic times they have come to see their future resting in the hands of one woman. The political developments and the tone of the politicians' speeches are all too familiar. They have heard it all before. And they are convinced that despite the arguments for keeping the islands as part of the West's defences against Russia's mighty "Blue water navy" and the promise of mineral and oil riches in the Antarctic, they will indeed be "sold down the river" as soon as it is convenient.

This may not be true, but the Falklanders believe it.

Mrs Thatcher reflected their feelings in her Christmas message to them when she said: "I regret that at the recent General Assembly so many of our friends proved unwilling to face up to the real issues at stake. They were content to have self determination for themselves, but not all of them were content or prepared to vote for it for the people of the Falkland Isles."

Below: Off duty servicemen admiring the memorial plaque in Port Stanley dedicated to the memory of Task Force members who lost their lives in the battle to regain control of the Falklands. Right: The Falklands flag is raised aloft during a parade held in Stanley. Garrison duties include ceremonial occasions.

Chapter 2

LAND WAR: NATO VERSUS WARSAW PACT

Facing each other across the North German plain are two of the World's best-equipped and deadliest forces – the armies of NATO and the Warsaw Pact. This is the crucible where East meets West, where the spark of a global conflict could so easily be ignited.

German Leopard MBT under vigilant cover in a cornfield.

Easily the most powerful and mobile concentrations of conventional forces in the world are massed facing each other across the Inner German Border (IGB) – the frontier between East and West Germany. The soldiers of both sides are more heavily and completely equipped for battle than any others and their weaponry is refined, modernised and added to year after year. In support of the swarms of Armoured Fighting Vehicles (AFVs) which protect infantry and gunners as well as tank crews there are thousands of tactical strike aircraft, fleets of helicopters and all sorts of specialists from Air Defence regiments to Signals Intelligence teams. It is an awesome concentration of military power and it is not simply devoted to warlike display. Both sides constantly exercise, hold large-scale manoeuvres and plan for the day when they may clash with each other.

Both the Warsaw Pact forces in the east and the NATO allies in the west are powerful but the strength of the Pact is markedly the greater. The chief member of the Pact is the Soviet Union and it holds a forceful and complete authority over the other members: Bulgaria, Czechoslovakia, the German Democratic Republic, Hungary, Poland and Romania. This authority may be resented and occasionally flouted (Romania does not hold joint manoeuvres with other Pact countries) but it has great advantages. Almost all equipment is Soviet supplied and the large forces which the East Germans,

Poles, Czechoslovaks and Hungarians might contribute to any Pact offensive across the IGB have the same scale of equipment and method of operation as well as being subordinate to Soviet command. No such compatibility of equipment or method exists on the NATO side where West Germany, Italy and Britain have major indigenous armaments industries which occasionally rival that of the United States. In addition to this the US may be the acknowledged leader of the alliance but it is an alliance of truly sovereign states with marked national sensitivities and one signatory, France, has taken no part in joint planning or military co-operation for two decades.

Besides the advantage of uniformity the Pact and, indeed, the Soviet Union alone enjoys a very considerable superiority in numbers. The extent of this superiority is difficult to judge. It is hard to equate tanks with numbers of anti-tank systems or a heavy gun with one of lighter calibre. Calculations as to how many of the Soviet Union's 50 tank divisions and 136 motor rifle divisions would be available and equipped for an offensive in their Western Theatre also vary greatly. All in all a preponderance of 3 to 1 is a fairly respectable estimate and 2 to 1 is highly conservative.

Below: The M-2 Bradley Infantry Fighting Vehicle is not only an effective means of delivering personnel to the battlefield, but also carries a potent anti-tank capability in its turret-mounted TOW missile launcher.

Above: German-built Leopard C1 tank of the Canadian reinforcing brigade attached to NATO forces in Europe. Equipment standardization is a NATO strength.

The figures behind the idea that the Warsaw Pact will be twice as strong as NATO are, like all others, an informed guess. It is reasonable to assume that the Warsaw Pact could put 17,500 Main Battle Tanks (MBTs) into action within three days and that NATO could field 7,000 to meet them. At the same time the Pact would deploy 7,500 artillery pieces to NATO's 2,700, 47 divisions totalling 950,000 men to NATO's 32 divisions totalling 780,000 men and 2,700 Pact front line fixed wing aircraft against 1,150 of their NATO equivalents. Only in armed helicopters (400 to 150) and Anti-Tank Guided Weapon (ATGW) launchers (4,000 to 1,200) would NATO be superior. These figures are alarming enough for NATO generals but the picture would grow even blacker within thirty days of mobilisation. By then there would be 30,000 Pact MBTs to take on 10,000 from NATO and 17,000 Pact artillery pieces to outgun NATO's 4,000 while 120 Pact divisions would be in battle with 60 NATO divisions. The picture would have improved slightly as far as combat fixed wing aircraft were concerned, but would have deteriorated as regards armed helicopters and hardly changed in numbers of ATGW launchers.

Local Pact superiority

At first sight this overall superiority of more than 2 to 1 would not seem to be overwhelming but it does not con-

vey the full reality of local advantage. The conventional military wisdom states that an attacker must have a 3 to 1 advantage over a defender if he is to win but this equation does not refer to an overall advantage so much as an advantage in the decisive sector. However one calculates the relative strengths it still remains obvious that the Pact can maintain pressure all along the NATO line and still bring odds of 10 to 1 to bear in at least five 'breakthrough sectors'. In addition to this it must be remembered that the Pact forces plan to attack while NATO plans to defend so the Pact will have the dangerous power of dictating the course of the battle in its earliest stages. They will be able to concentrate where they wish to do so while NATO must remain dispersed until the 'breakthrough sectors' or axes of the attack have been clearly identified.

This great numerical advantage has been taken into account fully by the Russian strategic planners and the operational experts who have designed the type of forces they deploy. In the 1950s and 1960s the idea was for the Pact forces to 'take out' most opposition with tactical nuclear weapons and then simply motor through the light resistance that remained in a highly mobile armoured mass. The armoured vehicles would give the attackers protection against radiation so this period saw the beginning of forces in which all arms – tanks, infantry and guns – were armoured as well as mechanised. When the idea of the tactical nuclear strike was abandoned because of the likelihood of devastating NATO retaliation these immensely powerful armoured masses

remained to suggest to the Soviet planners that their strength still lay in a quick and overwhelming attack.

As far as is known the present Soviet plans are to burst through the defence at a number of points and for their forces to drive the attack to the full depth of the objective (which would mean the Channel coast) as quickly as possible. To do this they have created two types of division: tank and motor rifle. Each division is divided into four regiments (the equivalent of four brigades in the west) and every regiment contains a quota of tanks, infantry and guns. The proportions vary with division types so that a tank division will deploy 330 tanks and a motor rifle division will have 240 – which is still an extraordinarily high establishment of tanks. All the divisional arms will be highly mobile and armoured so that the infantry in their tracked BMP fighting vehicles, the gunners in their self-propelled guns (SPG) and every supporting group from air defence specialists to signals experts in their tracked vehicles can stream forward at the pace of the tanks with reasonable protection from NATO small arms and artillery.

The Pact plan is to punch a hole in the NATO forward defence in a number of places and then to drive division after division, army after army, through these holes. Once the breakthrough had been accomplished this overwhelming force would sweep forward along narrow corridors or axes of advance to the full depth of the objective. From time to time powerful battalion sized groups of all arms would swing aside from the line of march to sieze minor objectives and mount raids that would confuse the NATO defenders and disrupt their attempts to strike back. These subsidiary attacks are very much regarded as diversions designed to assist the prime objective of keeping the main force moving rapidly along the axis of attack and keeping its momentum going by refusing to be bogged down by a defender. To some extent the main spearhead would be rolling forward along a prepared path because the whole 300 kilometre axis of each attack would be under some sort of sustained assault from the moment hostilities began: commandos would be air lifted ahead to seize vital objectives and bombers would disrupt the movement of enemy reserves.

Resources available to tackle UK

Although the Soviet commanders probably do not imagine that their armoured strike will cross the channel, they have large quantities of other forces to overwhelm NATO rear areas as distant as the ports and airfields of

Left: The Soviet Union has highly-trained, specialist forces called Spetsnaz. The Spetsnaz are trained to land secretly by air or sea to sabotage vital military installations, ports, centres of communication, military depots and other bases that would be suitable targets for such covert attacks. Speztsnaz targets in Europe are likely to be assassinations of senior politicians and army officers, nuclear munitions dumps, NATO oil pipelines and likely choke points for reinforcements of NATO front line forces. This trooper wears para smock with standard webbing, and carries an AK 47 assault rifle.

Above: The Warsaw pact will undoubtedly deploy large numbers of heavily armed attack helicopters such as this Mil-24 Hind. The Soviet Union currently has over 1100 Hinds of various types available as ground support for its troops in the European theatre. The Hind gunships have proved effective in Afghanistan.

Britain. For this type of operation the Soviet Union maintains 7 Airborne divisions (each one containing three regiments of paratroops, one artillery regiment and an anti-aircraft battalion), some 8 air assault brigades (each containing three rifle battalions with mortar, anti-aircraft and anti-tank support troops) and no fewer than 16 brigades of its highly trained special forces – the famous *Spetsnaz*. A rough indication of the strength of these forces is that each Soviet airborne division contains some 7,000 men so that the total number of troops that could be used for operation behind the NATO front is very large indeed.

The actual business of smashing through the NATO defence and maintaining an advance on a very narrow front would be achieved by the echelonment of the Pact armies. The first echelon are the armies based in East Germany and these could be hammering at the NATO line within hours of a standing start. Each division would be allocated a specific task which, if it was a breakthrough division, would be an attack down an avenue a

The European Front

Map showing the concentration, location and probable lines of attack in the event of an East-West European conflict. Even though these details are known, and extensively planned for, a real engagement would be unpredictable in its outcome once the effects of terrain hazards and the ultimate threat of the nuclear option – tactical as well as strategic – come into play. At present, this sector of Europe contains the heaviest concentration of men and military might in the world.

In the illustration, the aircraft symbols represent military air bases, the tanks; armoured divisions, the APCs; mechanised infantry divisions, the paratroops; airborne divisions, and the guns are artillery units.

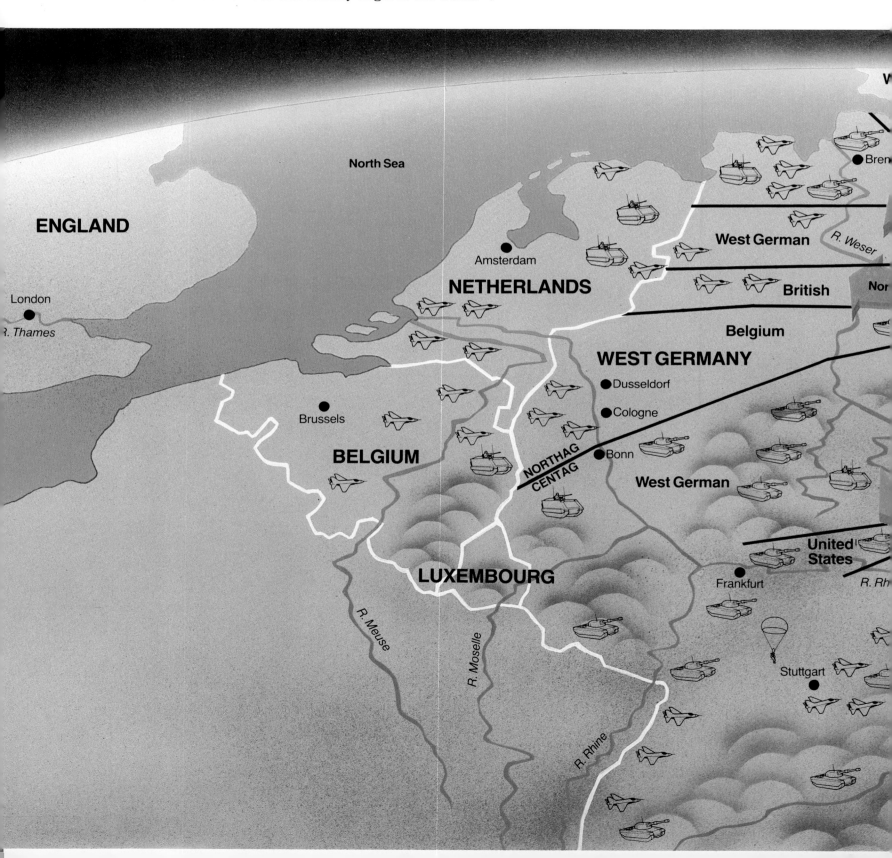

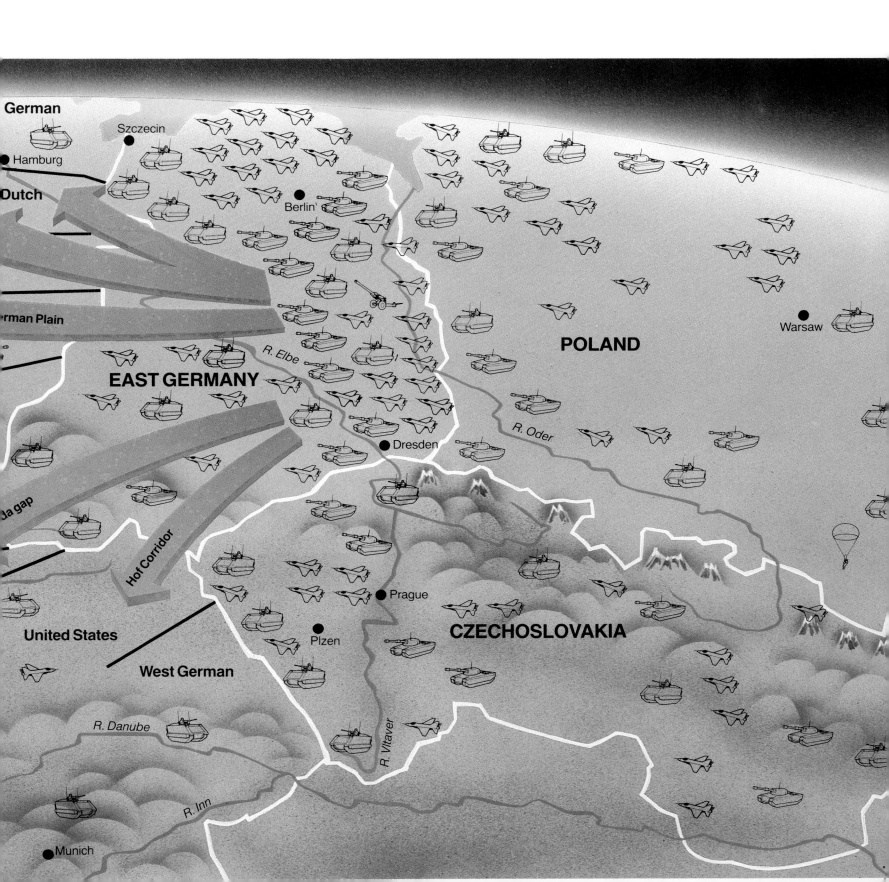

German

Szczecin

Hamburg

Dutch

rman Plain

R. Elbe

EAST GERMANY

Berlin

POLAND

Warsaw

R. Oder

Dresden

da gap

Hot Corridor

United States

West German

Prague

CZECHOSLOVAKIA

Plzen

R. Danube

R. Vltaver

R. Inn

Munich

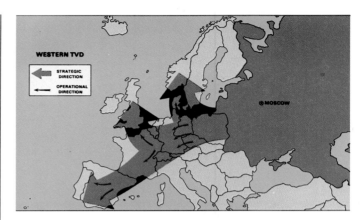

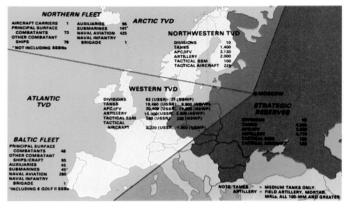

Above left: An M-109 self-propelled Howitzer of the Belgian army. Currently, work is underway to upgrade both the munitions and, in some cases, the artillery pieces themselves of the NATO forces. Below: An M-46 130 mm standard field-gun of a Soviet Guards artillery battery in action during Warsaw Pact exercises in Europe. Above: The map references TVD stand for the Russian *Teatr Voennykh Deistvii*. The upper map shows the general and specific thrust lines of a Warsaw Pact invasion of Northern and Central Europe, with a speculative thrust into Spain. The illustration below shows the distribution of Soviet military and Naval assets as they affect Western Europe.

few kilometres wide. The task would be pursued until it had been successfully achieved or the division had been exhausted and destroyed by the battle. If the latter happened the remnants of the division would be withdrawn and a fresh division immediately fed into the attack. Any success could be exploited immediately by a powerful 'operational mobile group' (OMG) held in army reserve. Once the first echelon had started to bite into the defence the OMG could be used to smash clean through the NATO line to give a clear run to the second echelon troops pouring forward from their base areas in Poland and Western Russia. The intended effect is of an unstoppable war machine which will deliver a pitiless succession of blows at a few chosen points. The theory is that sheer concentration of force guarantees success.

Beyond this too is the concept of an inflexible and iron control of the battle by the Soviet High Command – Divisional units do not have their own supply vehicles going backwards and forwards to replenish exhausted

Above: BMP-1 mechanised infantry combat vehicles (MICVs) of the Soviet Naval Infantry during manoeuvres. The vehicles carry a crew of three plus eight infantry men.

stocks but are supplied from the rear at the dictate of senior commanders. In theory each division goes into battle with enough supplies to fight its battle and reach its objective. When the battle is over successful divisions will be resupplied by convoys rolling forward from the rear and unsuccessful divisions will be ignored or withdrawn. By this 'top-down' resupply system the Soviets show clearly their intention to reinforce success with a maximum concentration of available resources.

Pact performance below potential

At first sight the Pact forces would seem to be assured of success. Their great advantage in numbers coupled with their very complete mobility and the fact that all commanders of regimental level and above are trained to a high degree of skill in managing fluid, encounter battles would seem to make them an unstoppable force. But, even before one looks at the preparations NATO have made to receive them, certain weaknesses can be seen. The first one is that there may not be enough infantry even in a motor rifle division to cover the tank spearheads from the tank-hunting infantry of a determined enemy. Just as likely to imperil success are the acknowledged weaknesses of the Soviet Army which consistently manages to produce mediocre performances despite its vast potential.

The prime weakness is in the quality of Soviet com-

Above: M-1 Abrams Main Battle Tanks of the US Army on manoeuvres. They form part of the 61st Armored (Tiger) Brigade flown in from the USA to man their tanks which are pre-prepared and left in Europe for their arrival.

manders below regimental level. Given that the best manpower is taken by the elite airborne and *Spetsnaz* organisations and many good quality non-commissioned officers are absorbed by the vast training establishment needed to instruct a largely conscript force, only the less able remain in the front line units. Officers as senior as battalion commanders appear to be of equally indifferent quality. Intelligence suggests that they combine lack of initiative with an unwillingness to report an unfavourable situation for fear of being blamed for it. An admission of this general incompetence is contained in the acknowledgement that the Soviet commander needs 18 to 22 hours to launch a 'hasty battalion attack' where his western counterpart will make do with two.

This poor quality at the lower levels has been one of the reasons behind the Soviet plan of attack. Selected senior commanders who have been through special academies have a far higher level of skill and leadership which is why they insist on such rigid control of the battle from the rear. That there may be problems in this can be illustrated by the fact that the massive size of Soviet military organisations places them at the very limits of operational control. A single Soviet tank army heading west at normal speed would have its head near Aachen as its tail cleared Berlin. With its usual share of additional support troops, commandos and other specialists its head would be nearer the Belgian coast. As

Right: British Paras on a training exercise in Northern Norway. These exercises are aimed at securing the reinforcement of NATO's northern flank. Below: T-72 Main Battle Tanks of the Soviet Army during Warsaw Pact exercises in Eastern Europe.

the Soviets could expect to deploy 12 armies on the Central Front in Europe the problems of control would be enormous.

There is also a slight question mark over the quality of Soviet equipment. The ubiquitous BMPs which carry the rifle sections and the SAM and signals support sections were considered remarkably potent machines on their first appearance. In 1973 however they proved highly vulnerable to the attack of all sorts of anti-armour weapons. There may be some problem with the tank masses too. Quite a large number of the tanks issued to Pact forces in Europe are T-64s and there is some tacit acknowledgement that they are unsatisfactory in the fact that their production has been discontinued. Most Pact forces now have the similar T-72 (also confusingly called the T-74 by the Soviets and the T-80 by the Americans in its latest variants which use the highly protective laminated armour). The T-74/80 is certainly a highly effective MBT although most NATO soldiers would prefer their latest generation MBTs – the American M1 Abrams, the German Leopard 2 and the British Challenger.

It would not do however to make too much of these Soviet weaknesses. The giant may have an Achilles heel but it would be hard enough to find it and exploit it in combat. The overall impression given by the Pact forces is one of overwhelming might and it is this which confronts NATO planners as they review their rather slender resources for the defence of the European theatre.

As far as can be foreseen NATO expects to fight for Europe on three fronts. In the North the Soviet Union can deploy two armies totalling 6 tank and 8 motor rifle divisions against a Norwegian Army which is rather differently organised but probably amounts to about 2 divisions only although Norwegian reserves would make up about four more divisions. These troops could be very quickly reinforced by British and Dutch marines in something like divisional strength while American troops would also become available at a later stage. Given the great defensive strength of the Norwegian countryside the Northern Front is a cause of some anxiety but NATO commanders believe it will hold.

NATO in the Med
On Europe's Southern Flank are the Mediterranean countries. Here Greece and European Turkey face a manageable number of Pact troops with no Soviet troops actually stationed on their borders. The Soviet Army is so powerful however that it is possible to imagine it generating a threat in the Balkans or, indeed, of directly attacking Italy through the territory of non-aligned countries such as Austria and Yugoslavia. On the whole this scenario is regarded as possible but unlikely so the main focus of concern lies along the Central Front – from the Alps to the Baltic. Here the chief concern is to halt the Pact at the IGB and defend Denmark. It is here that 12 Soviet armies and numerous divisions

Above: British Army Challenger tank during the Lionheart exercise in Europe in 1984. It is intended to equip the British Army of the Rhine (BAOR) with an additional Challenger-equipped regiment within the next two years.

supplied by Pact allies pose an immediate threat which can be quickly reinforced by further armies from Western Russia.

Not only are the numbers against NATO but the ground also poses difficulties. The greatest difficulty is political. Because of the great damage and heavy civilian casualties that would occur in the battle areas, the West German government has demanded that NATO should adopt a shallow forward defence. All the NATO countries pay at least lip-service to this ideal but there is widespread concern that it robs them of the space to manoeuvre. Indeed, even if the whole area east of the Rhine were allowed to NATO forces as a battle ground, it would still lack operational depth for the campaign of manoeuvre that most modern generals see as the best counter to the superior strength of the Warsaw Pact.

This argument over the type of defensive campaign that should be mounted is another area of NATO weakness. In the 1960s and 1970s the old fashioned doctrine of flexible response held sway. The idea of this was that NATO would fight a furious forward defensive campaign for as long as possible to give the politicians an opportunity to negotiate an end to the crisis. If the politicians failed and the superior forces of the Pact brought NATO to the brink of defeat, the response would escalate and nuclear weapons would be used. Nowadays this strategy has been largely abandoned as a nuclear exchange seems a less than credible way of solving a political crisis and as NATO generals have begun to believe that defeat is not absolutely inevitable. There are still not enough NATO troops to have a strong chance of winning the battle but there is an outside chance. The difficulty is that the NATO nations have no coherent strategy to follow and the most likely way for a less numerous but agile force to defeat a numerous but ponderous foe is through a war of manoeuvre in depth which is expressly forbidden by the doctrine of forward defence.

As an illustration of the differences between the various approaches of the NATO contingents on the Central Front it is instructive to look at the extremes. One nation above all others seems to scorn manoeuvre theory and to have prepared itself for an annihilating battle of attrition – the British. British tanks are heavily armoured and have powerful guns but are comparatively slow. The same goes for the established fleet of armoured infantry carriers and also the lack of mobility in air defence units. There are signs that this is beginning to change but the British Army's capacity for a fast-moving war of manoeuvre has historically been low. Its great strength is in the calm determination of its smallest sections and the amazingly high quality of most junior leaders. The great weakness is in the poor training of junior officers which robs it of that sureness that the Army will work well above the lowest tactical level. This is possibly a major factor determining the fondness for attrition.

Under attrition theory the British Army will seize and hold on to vital positions astride an enemy axis of advance across the North German Plain. As it will be essential to the Pact to take these positions its forces will be forced into costly assaults against prepared defences. If attrition is to be effective Pact casualties would be so heavy that their forces would be 'written down' to the point where the British could advance cautiously to another position vital to them and force them to renew their attacks until they were further 'written down' and exhausted. This process could be repeated time and again until the Pact armies were destroyed.

Numerical disadvantage

In all fairness not even the most hopeful British commanders could imagine that their small force of a half dozen divisions could destroy the two Pact armies of fourteen divisions that they are likely to encounter. However the British Army of the Rhine might just be able to impose disruptive delay and unacceptable casualties by a skilful use of ground and resources. The ground they have been assigned to defend is 'in princi-

ple' an open plain which offers a clear road for tank armies through Brunswick and Hanover to the Netherlands. In fact the area is very different from the steppes and plains over which the Warsaw Pact normally conducts its larger exercises. It is indeed broken up with marsh, woodland, waterways and, increasingly, modern housing developments. All these obstacles would be seeded with heavily armed British infantry deploying ATGW. In support they would have the Chieftain tanks of their armoured regiments and, although Chieftains are not the most mobile of MBTs, they are among the most powerful tank killers in the NATO inventory.

It is highly unlikely that the oncoming Soviet forces would be able to brush through such opposition or that their SPG would be able to drive soldiers of such known determination off their positions. This would mean a series of major delays as the Pact infantry were forced to dismount from their vehicles and clear through the obstacles on foot. Each time they did so they would be vulnerable to local counter-attacks from the British reserve armoured formations. All told the British tactics would be likely to disrupt the tempo of the attackers and degrade their eventual performance by killing or pinning down large numbers of their infantry. This would amount to a very doughty performance but not a war-winning one because no large mobile reserve exists to tear into the enemy once he has been thrown off balance by the unexpectedly heavy resistance. The predictable end would be that the British would be forced into an increasingly disorganised withdrawal before being submerged under the successive waves of a numerically superior enemy.

Under the circumstances it is hardly surprising that the other NATO contingents have decided against attrition and have been more and more attracted by the idea of a war of manoeuvre. A debate on the subject has been raging for the last six years and it is not over yet. The arguments are wide ranging but the most universally popular model of a general who repeatedly defeated far superior forces by the adroit use of manoeuvre is Hitler's Field Marshal Fritz Erich von Manstein. He had an uncanny knack of allowing a Russian breakthrough to develop until it was ripe for him to send his reserve Panzertruppen racing at some vulnerable point along the outstretched enemy armoured tentacle to *die Stossgruppe aus den Angeln zu heben* (lift it off its hinges). In other words he would ram his own armoured force into the area behind the leading Soviet elements and in front of their follow up elements – thereby cutting them off. Again and again this succeeded in reducing a vastly superior enemy to chaos and inflicting heavy defeats on his offensive forces.

For forces likely to face similarly powerful Russian attacks a generation later the power of this manoeuvre has its attractions. For the Germans who provide the largest NATO contingent (and, indeed for the Dutch, who are very similarly equipped to the Germans and share many of their ideas) have as strong a tradition for fighting a war of manoeuvre as the British have for a

Top left: Soviet SA-8 surface-to-air missile launch vehicle designed to provide advancing Pact forces with an integrated defence system. **Top right:** Roland Air Defence Vehicle of the 1st Panzer Regiment crossing a floating bridge over the Danube during exercises in West Germany. **Above left:** The German concept of battle by manoeuvre places great emphasis on engineering operations. German Pioneers bridge the Danube in just 75 minutes. **Above right:** A Marder Armoured Fighting Vehicle of the Panzer Grenadiers crossing a speedily-erected pontoon bridge in Germany. West Germany is capable of placing all its front line Infantry under the protection of armoured vehicles for manoeuvre and attack. **Right:** Leopard tanks of the 29th Panzer Brigade roll by during a Feldparade to celebrate the end of a field training exercise and the 30th anniversary of the founding of the modern Bundeswehr. The Germans provide the largest contingent to NATO forces in northern Europe, but having no nuclear capability.

battle of attrition. The trouble with the theory is that the policy of forward defence does not allow NATO defenders the space to follow Manstein's practice. He had the vast open areas of the Ukraine to lure the enemy columns forward until the moment came to strike but his successors in the Bundeswehr have no such luxury. They will also be temperamentally inclined towards forward defence because they will be fighting for their own country.

In the event the Germans have come to a conclusion that is only partially satisfactory. The stated idea is for a stubborn defence well forward but for reserves to be kept ready for at least local counter-attacks to take the enemy in flank or rear. These are rather modest ambitions when set beside the fact that the Germans still hold to their time-honoured belief that maximum force should be concentrated on a single decisive point – the *schwerpunkt* that Manstein and others exploited so successfully. The truth may well be unstated for political reasons and it may be that the Germans will look for depth of manoeuvre by driving eastward across the Inner German Border and biting at the tail of the Pact armies. The expression of such ideas is politically unacceptable but there is evidence that they are current in a number of NATO military discussions.

NATO members tactics vary

Just as the British and the Germans seem to cling to their traditional methods of making war, so too do the Americans. They have two powerful corps formations stationed in southern Germany and a third corps due to reinforce the north in time of war. It is unsurprising that an American appraisal of the situation has arrived at a technical solution. Their logical conclusion is that the chief danger facing NATO is posed by the great masses of Soviet and Pact armour. Some years ago they decided to turn this into a disadvantage by perfecting a number of ways of attacking armour. In addition to this their plan was to extend this attack deep into the enemy positions so that the follow up elements would suffer long before they reached the Forward Edge of the Battle Area (FEBA). To do all this they have relied on their mastery of technology.

Of all the forces likely to be involved in battle on the Central Front, the Americans are the most lavishly equipped. Their surveillance and signals satellites circle ceaselessly overhead and aircraft carrying complicated ground and air surveillance equipment are constantly

Right: US Army Hueycobra ground attack helicopters operating with a Belgian Corps, designed to blunt an armoured thrust.

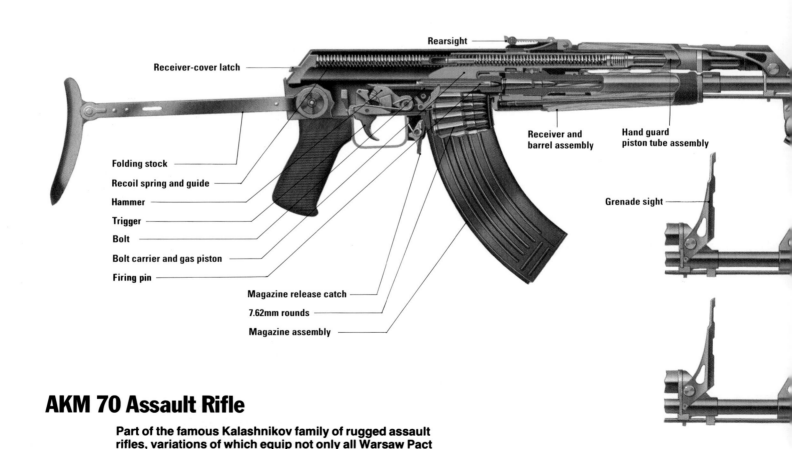

Rearsight

Receiver-cover latch

Receiver and barrel assembly

Hand guard piston tube assembly

Folding stock

Recoil spring and guide

Hammer

Trigger

Bolt

Bolt carrier and gas piston

Firing pin

Grenade sight

Magazine release catch

7.62mm rounds

Magazine assembly

AKM 70 Assault Rifle

Part of the famous Kalashnikov family of rugged assault rifles, variations of which equip not only all Warsaw Pact and Soviet backed armies, but also the forces of many non-aligned nations and organizations throughout the world.

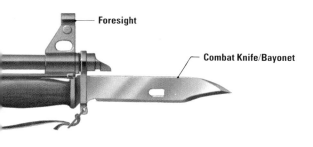

Foresight

Combat Knife/Bayonet

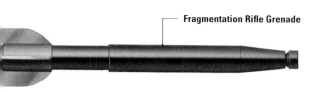

Fragmentation Rifle Grenade

Anti-tank Rifle Grenade

airborne. In time of war it would be the task of those watching instrument banks to pinpoint the whereabouts of enemy armour and particularly its areas of concentration. This would mean not only the points on the FEBA where the Pact was attempting a breakthrough but on the hidden crossing points of the rivers Elbe, Oder, Vistula and perhaps even as far east as the Dnieper where the second echelon forces would be hurrying forward to join the battle. Wherever there was bunching or queueing target areas would have been discovered.

Recent research has given the United States admirable weapons to use against such Pact force concentrations. Apart from manned aircraft there are accurate cruise missiles which can deliver a destructive payload at great distances. The payload itself would probably be a cluster bomb which would scatter anti-armour bomblets above the target or spread anti-armour minelets along the route forward. Already developed and coming into service are terminally guided munitions with sensors that will actually seek out armoured vehicles for destruction. This is the 'Strike Deep' concept which is designed to make it a bitter and disagreeable experience for Pact forces to move or deploy even hundreds of kilometres behind the FEBA.

The great cost of the weaponry needed for 'Strike Deep' has caused some NATO controversy. It has been suggested that the Americans were too concerned with the attack on the second echelon forces and would be distracted by that objective while the first echelon and the OMG would be tearing through their ground forces. In fact the criticism is not valid because the United States has also devoted a certain amount of resources to the attack of armour at relatively close quarters. Very large numbers of helicopters armed with ATGW and the only ground attack aircraft exclusively designed to destroy tanks would be an invaluable support to the ground troops trying to stem a major assault. It is simply that helicopters and slow flying aircraft armed with gatling cannon are not obviously technically as advanced or expensive as the 'Strike Deep' Weapons; it seems less US effort has gone into the close support battle.

Airland concept vital

In every aspect of the struggle it is apparent enough that it is from the air as much as on the ground that the Americans intend to contain an assault. This is not a new development and the idea of using the air as another medium for manoeuvre as well as for attack was current during the Vietnam war. From this has stemmed the American concept of the 'airland' battle as being a more realistic description of complete land warfare. In their movement down this road they have reinstated Air Cavalry Assault Brigades (ACAB) on their 1986 establishment. The idea is that their helicopter fleet could deploy a significant force in an operationally advantageous position beyond the FEBA while other NATO countries still tend to think of the helicopter as useful only for quick deployment behind the FEBA.

With all this new weaponry and the lavish provision of

Top: A-10 tank-busting Thunderbolts of the USAF. Underwing armaments include 4 Maverick Air-to-Ground Missiles. The aircraft's 30mm cannon can reach an astonishing 4000 rounds a minute. Below: Soviet Mil-24 Hind ground-attack helicopter gunship.

air and land vehicles that give exceptional mobility, the Americans have moved furthest from the more static warfare that the British are still stuck with. Any force attacking the US Army could expect to come under fire long before it reached the FEBA. Once there he would find no rigid defence but would be blocked in by mobile units while he came under heavier and even more precise fire from guns as well as aircraft. His every movement would be watched by surveillance sensors and he would come under attack in flank and rear by armoured units closely informed about his dispositions.

Between the British and the Americans one can run the gamut of all the other allies actually under NATO command. American equipment is better and more plentiful than that of any other nation although the Dutch and Germans are not far behind. The British and Belgians are the least well equipped although the British are gradually improving their position. While the British

Army may be materially hamstrung by thirty years of defence cuts, it is still at the top of the league for enthusiasm and training because it is an all-volunteer professional organisation with the extraordinarily high moral conferred on it by its clannish regimental system. The Americans too are professionals but their army is far larger so that it needs a larger training establishment and the rewards of civilian employment for competent men can be very high indeed. This combines to deny the front line US Army the services of good senior non-commissioned officers where their organisation is weak. The Germans too have this lack for exactly the same reasons and a large part of their force is also conscripted.

The fighting quality of an army need not be greatly degraded because it contains conscripts. Obviously well trained volunteers will have an edge but well motivated conscripts can be very effective. It is a pity therefore, from the point of view of combat readiness, that the Dutch and Belgian conscripts serve for such a short space of time (for the Dutch it can be only 14 months and the Belgians may do as little as 8 months). Of the other contingents immediately involved the Danes will hope to defend their peninsula with poorly equipped conscripts serving 8 months and the Canadians will bring a well-equipped heavy brigade group of excellently trained professionals to the struggle. All in all a confusing mixture of qualities even before one assesses the greatest enigma of all – the French.

The French enigma

France is a member of NATO but does not participate in the military structure of the alliance. There is a French Army corps in south west Germany but it is not under NATO command and it would take its orders from Paris in time of war. Behind it there are two more corps beyond the French border and a number more could be mobilised. This is a very formidable force which could be of the utmost importance to NATO in time of war but little is known of its intentions or tactics. From the fact that the French are provided with a fast, manoeuvreable MBT which may, indeed, be rather under-armoured, it can be assumed that they plan for a war of manoeuvre rather than a battle of attrition. It is unknowable however what, if anything, they would commit to battle on the Central Front and what they might reserve for the defence of their own border.

So, for the potential commander of the Central Front in time of war a difficult task of co-ordinating different national efforts can be expected. At first sight it might seem to be a hopeless endeavour but there is the example of very effective co-operation in one area. All the air forces – apart from that of the French – are well integrated and can be brought quickly to a high state of readiness. They have good early warning systems that can be linked into the command net and they also expect to win their battle. Although Pact numbers are superior in absolute terms the NATO aircraft have a performance edge that should enable them to gain superiority within a few days of the outbreak of hostilities. This would be of crucial importance if the ground troops had been successful in channelling the oncoming enemy armour into 'choke points' that could be hammered from the air.

One of the most intriguing things about this co-operation between the air forces is that it copes with the differences between national methods of fighting. The Americans for instance intend to penetrate highly defended Pact air space by flying above the range of most defences. The British and Germans concern themselves with ground hugging raids that will fly under Pact radar. Not only is it recognised that both methods have a place but also that having more than one approach adds to the enemy's difficulties. This is a hopeful example for the increasing emphasis on co-ordination for the ground armies.

Plan and counterplan

The Soviet Union as leader of the Pact has worked out an elaborate operational procedure and detailed plans for an assault on the West. For the West to plan its defence would not be possible but it would be helpful if a common approach to operational procedure could be adopted. The conduct of operations comes in that grey area between strategy and tactics and could probably be defined simply as battle command of large forces. Most NATO soldiers now see the need for coherence and talks are advancing steadily down that road. Opinion is hardening – even among the British – that only a war of manoeuvre is likely to defeat the offensive threatened from the East. Decisions as to the size and type of the manoeuvre force are far harder to make. The Amer-

Below: AMX-30 Main Battle Tank of the French Army. Although a member nation, France's forces are separate from NATO, though she is in fact a member.

icans believe that a single corps should hold back enough reserves for an effective counter-attack but the Germans are more reluctant. For them such a manoeuvre would be almost tactical and hardly operational. They would like to see a strong command with a much larger reserve for the whole Front. While individual formations would mount local counter-attacks this army reserve would be launched at a theatre *schwerpunkt* to inflict a defeat on the Pact so great that it could not continue the battle.

At the moment NATO's diversity seems to be a weakness. However this would not necessarily be so if agreement on operational conduct is reached. For a war of manoeuvre there must be a holding force to confront and grapple with the enemy while the manoeuvre force prepares for the surprise strike at his weak point. Some national contingents – such as the British – are ideal holding force material while others – such as the French – can only be effective through manoeuvre and shock. The material for a highly effective and potentially victorious defence lies ready to hand.

At the moment however the odds favour a Pact victory in any clash. The largest opposing force is German and it is of undeniably high quality but too small to blunt and then disrupt the huge forces arrayed against it. The chief danger to the Pact today comes from American technology which can destroy at such distance behind the FEBA but it is certain that Soviet planners will have done as much as they can to neutralise this threat through electronic jamming and concealment. Until NATO concerts its various strengths it will almost certainly face defeat – if only because the confidence to sieze the initiative and counter-attack is not there. Sun Tzu, the great Chinese military master who lived before Christ was born explained that the side that believed it would lose could not win.

Chapter 3

REGIMENT IN REVIEW: ROYAL GREEN JACKETS

Made up of several individual Rifle Brigades which go back to the Peninsular War and earlier, the Royal Green Jackets are a Regiment noted for their traditions of quick-reaction, initiative and tactical skill as much on today's modern battlefield as in the heyday of the Baker Rifle.

Royal Green Jacket trooper with General Purpose Machine Gun (GPMG).

Mention of the name of The Royal Green Jackets summons up a number of immediate associations: to those who know it – and perhaps have belonged to it or the famous earlier Regiments now absorbed into it – regimental pride is inevitably the first such association. The Royal Green Jackets are the regimental product of a very long tradition. The various Regiments, Battalions and companies that have served under the aegis of what is now one large Regiment, have a history that goes back as far as 1741.

The Royal Green Jacket Regiment is also well known for its quality of light infantry soldiering, in particular its ingenuity in difficult circumstances; its strong contribution, through the military genius of a number of its early leaders, to the development of military tactics and philosophy; perhaps above all its renown for speed and daring in light infantry skirmishing and combat activities. The Regimental motto 'Swift and bold' is a modest self-description and one justified many times over throughout its history: 55 VCs tip the iceberg of thousands of other awards for bravery and gallantry in the colonial, tribal, frontier and World Wars in which it has played a prominent part. The motto is also an imperative to new recruits who quickly learn to take it to heart.

Not surprisingly, The Royal Green Jackets consider themselves something of an elite amongst the regular Armed Forces with the considered exception of the Parachute Regiment with whose training the Royal Green Jackets' closely compares. It is tough because the roles the Regiment is currently involved in at home, in BAOR and in Northern Ireland require toughness of mind and body. The present training is carried out at Winchester, a city associated with the Regiment since 1856 (or more precisely with the Regiments incorporated into this Regiment). The aim of this training is to produce a quick-thinking rifleman given easily to positive and daring action for which his physical and mental faculties are well-tuned.

Perhaps a key word in the training and operational philosophy of The Royal Green Jackets is adaptability. Like so many Regiments, The Royal Green Jackets have undergone massive changes in tactics, in formation, in numbers, in weaponry, over more than 200 years. Just as the prominent early leaders of such as the North American campaigns against the French and their Red Indian allies required radical changes in drill, dress and skirmishing tactics, the modern Regiment is fast adapting to a new highly mechanised role in the frontline Battle Groups of the European heartland of BAOR. There, versatility and speed are essentials.

Green Jackets join Light Infantry Brigade

In keeping with changing times, The Royal Green Jackets have only recently moved from the Peninsula Barracks in Winchester (named after the Peninsular War 1808-1814) where they have been based since 1858, to a brand new all-purpose depot, now also housing the other Regiment within the Light Infantry Division, The

Above: The deserted Peninsular Barracks at the Regiment's old headquarters in Winchester. Part of the site may be converted into a military museum.

Light Infantry Brigade. The latter Regiment only moved from its former traditional base in Shrewsbury in 1986 and together with the Royal Green Jackets enjoy the modern facilities of the Light Infantry Depot about two miles outside Winchester on the Andover Road.

The impact of the evacuation of the Peninsula Barracks over the last two years leaves the visitor to this extraordinary set of buildings with a sense of echoing space and an air of slight despond. The enormous main quadrangle, once thrilling with the high-pitched emissions of the drill sergeants, a site of colourful and proudly executed ceremonial march pasts and Passing-Out Parades, now looks mournfully empty. The large, handsome Victorian facade of the main building, with colonnades reinstalled from the original Christopher Wren building on this site, destroyed completely by fire on 21 December 1894, hides a great many once-busy offices and classrooms.

To the right of the main entrance to the barracks there is one building which is very much alive with the traditions of the Regiment. This is The Royal Green Jackets Museum housing an enormous collection of historiana including exceptional items like Sir John Moore's Gold Cross gained at the Peninsular Wars and a wide range of souvenirs, remnants and booty collected from far-flung battlefields for nearly 250 years. Amongst the flags, badges, medals, letters, documents, maps and weapons, the portraits of famous early leaders, with the notable Sir John Moore looming largest in the middle background, proudly regard the visitors.

One early leader whose presence is felt in this museum is Colonel Coote Manningham who was renowned particularly for his tenaciously-held views on

Above: Peninsular War hero General Sir John Moore in a contemporary illustration. He was killed in the famous retreat to Corunna.

military tactics, man-management and military philosophy generally. It was he who expounded the principle that men will fight together far better if they live and work together in the same fighting unit. This principle substantiates and in many ways underpins the regimental structure of the British Army and it is still held strongly today by the majority of Army personnel who have understood the value of its effect in practice. In fact, the life and activity of the 'Regiment' is fundamental to modern soldiering – the three famous fighting Regiments now constituting the Royal Green Jackets and discussed in detail below, testify to the strength of the philosophy of regimental comradeship and the importance of the character this brings with it.

The origins of the Regiment

The Royal Green Jackets were only formed as a large Regiment on 1 January 1966 by the amalgamation of 1st Green Jackets (the 43rd and 52nd), 2nd Green Jackets (The King's Royal Rifle Corps) and 3rd Green Jackets (The Rifle Brigade). These three Regiments, each singularly famous and often involved in the same historical campaigns, had been brigaded together before this to form The Green Jackets Brigade in 1958. The titles of these Battalions before this date were The Oxfordshire and Buckinghamshire Light Infantry (43rd and 52nd), The King's Royal Rifle Corps and The Rifle Brigade (Prince Consort's Own). There is still some temptation to refer to the present Battalions as 1st (OBLI), 2nd (KRRC), and 3rd (RB) but this is now not only inaccurate but anathema. The three present battalions of The Royal Green Jackets are simply the 1st, 2nd and 3rd and although their historical antecedents have been involved

in a great many changes in formation, dress, drill, numbers, appellation over two and a half centuries, these battalions now represent the one Regiment and the one regimental character – the versatile modern light infantry soldier.

This said, the origins of the Regiment are fundamental to the esteem in which it is held today as some account of the earlier, separate Regiments, will illustrate.

The Oxfordshire and Buckinghamshire Light Infantry

The Oxfordshire and Buckinghamshire Light Infantry was descended from the 43rd of Foot raised in 1741 and the 52nd of Foot raised in 1755; these Regiments were soon recognised as being local to Monmouthshire and Oxfordshire respectively. In 1803, together with the 95th (see below) they formed The Light Brigade under Sir John Moore and thereby became the first Regiments of the British Army to become Light Infantry. Subsequently, they fought with great distinction in the Peninsular War in Spain (remember the famous charge of the 52nd!). In common with all Rifle and Light Infantry Regiments they have a traditional reputation of great speed – with a marching pace of 140 to the minute (as against a standard of 120) and the march past at the double on ceremonial parades – a tradition that The Royal Green Jackets maintain today. In 1881, the 43rd

Above: Victorian recruiting poster for the Oxfordshire Light Infantry, part of Sir John Moore's Light Brigade.

and 52nd became one Regiment, The Oxfordshire Light Infantry, and this was retitled The Oxfordshire and Buckinghamshire Light Infantry in 1908. At the turn of the century this Regiment differed in one interesting respect from most others of the time: the Sovereign's health was never drunk in the Officer's Mess unless a representative of the Sovereign or member of the Royal Family was present to enjoy the toast.

The King's Royal Rifle Corps

The King's Royal Rifle Corps was first raised in 1755 as the 62nd (soon afterwards retitled the 60th) Royal American Regiment with recruits drawn largely from American colonists, many of whom were Swiss and German in origin. This Regiment alone comprised 4,000 men divided equally into four Battalions formed to save a critical situation in which the Red Indians were backed by the French against the British in a dispute over the ownership of Canada. At first, the formal tactics and conspicuous red coats of the British proved disastrous against the French and their native allies. The ground was very much against the British being thickly forested with large tracts of wasteland and bush. To match these conditions effectively the 1st Battalion, 60th Royal Americans adapted their style by wearing lighter, duller-coloured clothing, carrying lighter weapons, using simple drill words, open formations and rapid movement. In 1759, the 2nd and 3rd Battalions were prominent in the capture of Quebec under General Wolfe. It was the 60th who then took on the motto "Celer et Audax" which is the latin form of The Royal Green Jackets' present motto.

The Rifle Brigade

The early evolution of The Rifle Brigade is a history fraught with cross references, so one must tread carefully. In 1797 another Battalion of the 60th was raised, this being the 5th Battalion, and shortly afterwards a sister Green Jacket Regiment (the 95th), later The Rifle Brigade, was formed. These were the first two Rifle Regiments of the British Army and were known jointly as The Green Jackets. They were armed with a rifle, most probably the Baker 10½ lb long rifle, as opposed to the traditionally used smooth-bore musket used by the remainder of the Infantry.

The Green Jackets distinguished themselves in The Peninsular War with their green uniforms, special tactics and drills controlled by bugle calls. The French General Foy was much impressed with these riflemen and wrote from the Peninsula:

"The echoing sound of the rifleman's horn answered the double purpose of directing their movement and signalling those of the enemy."

This practice was kept up until 1897 by which time it had become anachronistic given the demands of the modern battlefield.

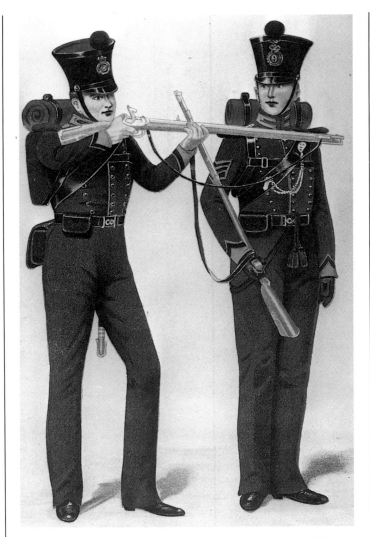

Above: Sergeant and Rifleman of the King's Royal Rifle Corps from the 1840's. Note percussion-cap rifle.

The Rifle Brigade was not actually so titled until 1816 but it was the Green Jacket Regiment (95th), raised by the early militarist Coote Manningham as an 'Experimental Corps of Riflemen' by drafts from 15 different regiments, that formed the kernel of this famous Regiment.

The men of this experimental brigade were dressed in dark green jackets and pantaloons and armed with the Baker rifle and sword. In the year of their formation, on 21 August 1800, they saw their first action at Ferrol and this date was subsequently celebrated as their Regimental birthday. In 1801 a detachment of the Corps took part as riflemen snipers in the naval battle of Copenhagen whence comes the naval crown at the base of The Royal Green Jackets' cap badge. In 1803 the experimental corps was renamed the 95th of the Rifle regiment and was brigaded, as mentioned above, under Sir John Moore. When, in 1816, the Corps was formally styled The Rifle Brigade it was removed from the Regiments of the Line and had the identity of a separate Regiment. From 1820 to 1852 the Duke of Wellington was Colonel-in-Chief of The Rifle Brigade and was succeeded by HRH The Prince Consort (hence the bracket 'Prince Consort's Own').

Organising for battle

To summarise even the name changes of these early Regiments is to negotiate pitfalls of protocol and certain ambiguities. But this brief excursion attests the manner in which the three principal components of today's Royal Green Jackets came together. A fascinating area in this history is the roles of the innovative leaders at the turn of the 18th and 19th centuries. Colonel Coote Maningham, already mentioned, was firm in his beliefs about military organisation and endeavours and gave a series of lectures on military subjects all delivered in a manner that made them seem gospel. Apart from helping to institute the theory of regimental comradeship as an essential, he was a stickler on all matters. He even sought to regulate the number of families allowed by officers and men in each of the Regiment's companies, stipulating that X number of wives were allowed for X number of men. Not stopping there, he decreed that in camp the women do all the washing for the men, but only the sergeants' wives were allowed to do the washing for officers. In general he had a humane view of the business of soldiering, which by any modern standards was reasonably barbaric at the time, and tempered firmness in discipline with the giving of encouragement and praise where it was deserved, or diplomatically effective.

The rifle, again probably the Baker, was evidently first issued to a company of the 60th and to one company of each of the other rifle battalions. The 10½ lb rifle was loaded at the muzzle and sighted for up to 200 yards. Bayonets could not be fixed so the riflemen carried swords – to this day they are referred to as swords in Rifle Regiments and are never carried fixed to rifles on regimental parades. The heaviest of the light guns used in the Peninsular War during the early days of the rifle regiments was the 9-pounder, with a range of up to 800 yards and no great accuracy.

The 19th Century Campaigns: Peninsular War

Among the troops under Sir Arthur Wellesley which landed in Spain in 1808 to help oppose Napoleon's armies at the beginning of the Peninsular War, were the 5th Battalion 60th and 2nd Battalion 95th Rifles. The 5th Battalion became attached in separate companies to various infantry brigades and were therefore present in some capacity at nearly every engagement in the long war until 1814.

The 2nd Battalion joined Sir John Moore at Corunna to make up a British force totalling 37,000 men. Napoleon arrived at Madrid with a force of almost 300,000 men (almost the size of the total number in the regular British Armed forces today). Chased hotly by Marshal Soult of the French Army, Moore had to retreat with no supplies and in appalling weather conditions back to Corunna. He lost 12,000 men on route. In a final engagement, the 2nd Battalion incurred many losses on the French forces and helped to defend Corunna whilst the rest of the British troops embarked to sail back to England. In this last battle Sir John Moore was killed and on the return journey a number of ships conveying the British troops home sunk in a storm. From an unpropitious beginning, seemingly against the odds, the British forces, in which the 5th Battalion 60th played a strong part, managed to acquit themselves with honour by the final battle of Toulouse on 10 April, 1814. After this battle there were only 9 officers and 250 rifles remaining in the 5th Battalion attached to Wellington's divisions.

In 1815 the various battalions of the 60th were designated the 60th Rifles and adopted a green colour dress. All the battalions of the 60th were then sent overseas in 1815 so this Regiment did not take part in Waterloo. The Royal Green Jacket's association with Waterloo stems from the actions of the 52nd and 95th who were particularly instrumental in the victory. It was the charge of the 52nd that finally broke the line of Napoleon's Imperial Guard. The 2nd Battalion of the 95th was afterwards given the honour of leading the victorious British Army into Paris after the surrender of the French forces.

Campaigns of Empire

During the remainder of the 19th Century all four Regiments – the 60th King's Royal Rifle Corps, the 43rd, the 52nd (these two Regiments becoming one in 1881) and the Rifle Brigade – fought in a long series of tribal, racial and frontier wars for Sovereign and Empire. They went to many parts of the world including Africa, Afghanistan, North America, Burma, Canada, China and the West Indies.

Below: Infantrymen of the 60th Rifles take up firing positions in a 19th century skirmish.

Above: Contemporary picture shows men of the 60th Rifles storming Delhi during the 1857 Indian Mutinies.

In the Crimean War in 1854 two battalions of The Rifle Brigade earned the peculiar distinction of being commended by an opposing commander. General Todleben said it was these riflemen who had caused the most damage to the Russians in the battle of Inkerman.

In fact, a number of Victoria Crosses went to these Regiments for formidable feats of gallantry at Alma, Sebastopol and for desperate attempts made by the 1st and 2nd Battalions of The Rifle Brigade to storm the Redan in 1855. By this time the Brigade had been rearmed with the then modern long Enfield rifle and bayonet. It was only in 1854 that the rest of the British Infantry had graduated from the famous old smooth-bore musket to the Minie Rifle.

Shortly after the Crimean War, all the Regiments were involved in the Indian Mutiny in 1857. The 52nd and 60th played particularly prominent roles in the Siege of Delhi and of the latter the Governor General wrote:

"The cheerfulness, steadiness and high qualifications as skirmishers of the 60th Rifles was beyond commendation."

During the colourful 19th Century years of war and peace, both on and off the battlefield, the Rifle Regiments developed and operated their own distinct methods of drill and firing formation. Notably, they eliminated any unnecessary words of command including the preliminary order 'Attention'; they never sloped arms but carried their rifles at the trail and never fixed 'swords' (bayonets) on ceremonial parades. The purpose behind this was to employ on the parade ground, and at all times, methods most suited to the battlefield. Quick marching (140 to the minute) and quick, silent drill brought with them quick thought and action.

The South African War 1899-1902

When fighting broke out between the British in South Africa and the Boers in the Transvaal all four regular Battalions of the 60th and The Rifle Brigade were involved for almost three years. During this period the British and the Empire put up a phenomenal 450,000 men and vast amounts of money. The Dutch Boers of the Transvaal proved exceptionally strong enemies, highly mobile and using great ingenuity but in the end the Empire held together and the experience gained showed how ill-prepared it was for the European War that followed 12 years later.

In the Defence of Ladysmith, the Relief of Ladysmith as well as at Bergendal, The Rifle Brigade saw a good deal of action. In 1899 at the battle of Colenso, Captain (later General Sir) Walter Congreve, RB, and Lieutenant the Hon. FHS Roberts, 60th, were both awarded the Victoria Cross for their attempt to save the guns. Captain Congreve was shot in the leg and had his horse shot from under him whilst Roberts was fatally wound-

50

ed. At Bergendal, despite the heavily fortified positions of the Boers, the 2nd Battalion The Rifle Brigade successfully broke through and captured them. One rifleman, RFn Durrant, was awarded a VC for his part in the action.

In the early part of the war, the 60th suffered severe punishment at the hands of the Boers. During the first battle of the war at Talana Hill Lieutenant Colonel Gunning led the assault of the 1st Battalion 60th which resulted in the complete defeat of the enemy but was himself killed during this assault. Four other officers were also killed out of the 17 officers present with eight others seriously wounded. Not surprisingly, the remnants of the 1st Battalion 60th, which also lost many NCOs and riflemen, joined forces with the 2nd Battalion and the 2nd Battalion The Rifle Brigade in the Siege of Ladysmith. The latter Battalion undertook an ingenious night sortie during this action. They silently advanced some 2,000 yards into the Boers' encircling lines, destroyed the 4.7in Howitzer on Suprise Hill which had caused them grievous damage until this point, then

Below: Riflemen and Maxim machine gun crew of the 1st Battalion of the King's Royal Rifle Corps in period pose at the turn of the century.

fought their way back through the Boer lines mainly by the adroit use of their bayonets.

In the Relief of Ladysmith the 3rd Battalion 60th gained a similar order of credit by capturing the Twin Peaks at the battle of Spion Kop. This action was achieved single-handed and without any artillery support. A historian of this war gives this account of the final episodes of the assault:

"At 5pm under cover of heavy fire from the left half battalion from Naval Guns, the right half fixed swords and rushed the eastern peak with a cheer. A few minutes later the left half were in possession of their peak also. Away galloped Burger's guns down the slope of the eastern peak, and the pompom from the slopes of the ridge now exposed to fire from above, down the hill and off the open ridge streamed Burger's commandos and Botha's reinforcements."

This objective won, the 3rd Battalion 60th had gained the key of the Boer's positions and the road to Ladysmith was open. At the very moment of victory the leader of the assault, Lieutenant-Colonel Buchanan-Riddell, invested with a large measure of moral and physical

courage, was killed on the summit. Major RCA Bewicke-Copley assumed command. Another well-barrelled officer, Major the Hon. EJ Montagu-Stuart-Wortley (later Major General, CB,CMG,MVO,DSO), took over the 2nd Battalion 60th, after the relief.

World War I

In the bloody period between 1914-1918 a great many riflemen were killed in the often fruitless sorts of action that characterised the Western Front. In addition to the main Battalions in existence at the end of the Boer Wars, the Great War saw an enormous expansion of numbers in all the Rifle regiments. The Oxfordshire and Buckinghamshire Light Infantry raised 15 Battalions. The 43rd (1st Battalion) spent the entire war in Mesopotamia and engaged in major actions at Ctesiphon and the long four-month defence at Kut-al-Amara. The 52nd fought continuously on the Western Front from August 1914 until the end of the war and, with other Battalions of the Regiment, added 27 Battle Honours to the already extensive Regimental Lists.

The new Battalions raised at this time were called Service Battalions coming as they did from civilians joining either voluntarily or through conscription and undergoing rapid rifle and infantry tactics training before being sent to the Front.

The 60th raised a total of 17 Service Battalions and added 71 Battle Honours to the Regimental Lists. During the War they lost 13,000 officers and riflemen with over 123,000 wounded. One action they took part in demonstrates how severely underated the German Army and equipment was: in the First Battle of Ypres (31st October-14th November) three companies of 1st Battalion 60th – Coys. 'B', 'C' and 'D' – were surrounded and overwhelmed on 2nd November. The remnants of the Battalion had to be withdrawn from battle on 18th November having lost five officers with a further 24 wounded and nine missing; 60 riflemen killed, 419 wounded and 490 missing – a staggering total of 1,027 men in six weeks!

But amidst the misery and slaughter, many riflemen achieved considerable feats of daring and a total of nine Victoria Crosses were awarded during the war. One account of a VC won by Captain JFP Butler is recorded in The London Gazette of 23rd August, 1915. It describes two acts of bravery for which the award was won in the previous year and reads almost like a synopsis of a slightly unbelievable heroic scenario in a film script:

"For most conspicuous bravery in the Cameroons, West Africa. On 17th November, 1914, with a party

Above: Riflemen of the 12th Battalion Rifle Brigade and of the 22nd French Division in hastily dug rifle pits covering a road during the Somme Crossings in March 1918.

of thirteen men he went into the thick bush and at once attacked the enemy, in strength about one hundred, including several Europeans, defeated them, and captured their machine gun and many loads of ammunition. On 27th December 1914, when on patrol duty with a few men, he swam the Ekam River, which was held by the enemy, alone and in the face of brisk fire, completed his reconnaissance on the further bank and returned in safety. Two of his men were wounded while he was actually in the water."

In the 3rd Battalion, 60th, a Rhodesian platoon was formed and there remained a strong affiliation through to the Second World War when a Rhodesian company had an outstanding record with the 1st Battalion 60th in the Western Desert.

The Rifle Brigade expanded to 21 Battalions during World War I, 12 of which saw active service with a total of 11,575 officers and men killed or dying of their wounds. This Regiment won 1,446 gallantry awards including 10 Victoria Crosses. One of the recipients was Major W.La T Congreve, the son of Major General Congreve who had won the VC in South Africa. Another record was achieved by Sergeant W Gregg VC, DCM,

MM, the first British soldier to win all three awards.

After The Great War, in 1919, a mixed company of 60th and The Rifle Brigade took part in a hopeful expedition to counter the Bolsheviks after the Russian Revolution had effectively established Bolshevik power.

The intention was to rally anti-Bolshevik elements of the population in and around Murmansk in North Russia and to deny the use of this ice-free port to the Germans. Despite the ambitious nature of the operation and the very difficult terrain and conditions in which the company was placed, many minor actions were expedited with invariable success by these already war-weary troops. The mixed company formed the rear-guard at Murmansk and were the last troops to embark for England when the inevitable British decision came to leave the Russians to their fate.

In the period between the Wars the regular Battalions of the 52nd, 60th and The Rifle Brigade were all in Ireland during 'the Troubles' – a role in which The Royal Green Jackets is still very much involved today.

World War II

Another fortaste of things to come: shortly before World War II, the 60th and The Rifle Brigade were chosen to form the first Motor Battalions which were designed to bring highly mobile infantry in their own vehicles in close support of armoured regiments. The most prominent and famous action of these Regiments

Above: Evacuation of remnants of the British Expeditionary Force on a cross-channel ferry just before the fall of Dunkirk in 1940. Oxfordshire and Buckinghamshire Light Infantry were among the last to get out. Below: A Rifle Brigade section covering a post in the hilly country surrounding the Quattara Depression, in World War II.

was undertaken by the 1st Battalion The Rifle Brigade, the 2nd Battalion The King's Royal Corps and 1st Battalion The Queen Victoria's Rifles (one of the five territorial battalions which played an important part in the war) in the defence of Calais in 1940. There, they held off repeated attacks by German tanks and infantry and made the evacuation of the British Expeditionary Force at Dunkirk both possible and successful. The 43rd and other Battalions of the Oxfordshire and Buckinghamshire Light Infantry were among the troops that managed to get away from Dunkirk.

The Western Desert

In North Africa, in early 1941, the 2nd Battalion The Rifle Brigade helped to bring about the final destruction of the 10th Italian Army at Sidi Saleh taking the surrender of 15,000 Italians including their C-in-C. Later that year, on 21st November, during the attack on Sidi Rezegh, Rifleman John Beeley gained a postumous VC for a piece of outright heroism which ensured victory for the 60th and sure death for himself. With many of the officers and men in his company pinned down and killed or wounded by heavy fire, he ran at point-blank range about 30 yards to the enemy gun position discharging the complete magazine of a Bren Gun, killing or wounding the entire enemy gun crew and silencing the anti-tank gun. Falling dead over his gun, hit in at least four places, Beeley had enabled his comrades to reach and capture their objective and take 700 prisoners.

In 1942 the 2nd Battalion 60th were instrumental in knocking out 32 enemy tanks whilst repulsing a German tank attack on the strategically vital Kidney Ridge in the battle of El Alamein. Later the 52nd were the first troops to land in Normandy in the preliminary airborne operations of June 1944; their action at Pegasus Bridge is recognised on The Royal Green Jackets cap badge. The 43rd followed shortly after the 52nd and were almost continuously in action until the end of the fighting. Other battalions of The Oxfordshire and Buckinghamshire Light Infantry distinguished themselves in Africa, Italy and Burma.

Since the war

During the years of 'peace' the British Army have been involved in about 90 campaigns or active operations. To list – or even know – them all is an unlikely task: Korea, Malaya, Indonesia, Aden, Brunei, Rhodesia and Oman are to mention a few of the better known overseas operations. In most cases The Royal Green Jacket Regiments, prior to and since the RGJs' official formation in 1966, have been either actively involved or on standby, bringing their increasingly mobile Infantry Battalions to bear against enemies in all types of terrain and climate. Since 1945 there have been a great many exercises involving the RGJs in every conceivable terrain including the Northern Flank of NATO, North America, many outposts of the commonwealth and other overseas training facilities. The RGJs in these years have fought, patrolled, exercised and further refined their historically distinguished role as frontline riflemen, all the while developing this role in motorised battalion formations. At the time of their formation, the 1st Battalion was stationed in Berlin, the 2nd was in Penang (Malaya) preparing for a second operational tour in Sbah, whilst the 3rd Battalion was in the process of handing over their operational area in Sarawak in preparation for their return to England. The principle of working and fighting together was all the while maintained although there is some degree of movement of men between the three interoperating Battalions. In 1966, the 2nd and 3rd Battalion were heavily involved in repulsing Indonesia's aggressive attacks against Malaysia in North Borneo and giving protection to the local inhabitants.

Reserve Forces

Also at the time of their incorporation as one large Regiment, the Regiment comprised three Battalions at the Rifle Depot and three Battalions of the Territorial Army – The Queen's Royal Rifles, The London Rifle Brigade and The Oxfordshire and Buckinghamshire Light Infantry (TA). On 1st April 1966 the Territorial Army was reorganised and replaced by the Volunteer Reserve which in the case of the Regiment consisted of the 4th

Right: Royal Green Jacket officer in No. 1 Dress. The name derives from the colour of the Rifle Brigades' uniforms during the Peninsular War. A traditional feature of the dress is the absence of brass buttons.

Above: Men of the 4th Battalion the Royal Green Jackets, a Territorial unit, training at their Otterburn facility in the UK. Territorials and Regulars share the same training programmes and locations.

(V) Battalion of The Royal Green Jackets with its HQ in Davies Street in London and companies in London, Oxford and Aylesbury.

Currently there are two TA Battalions, the 4th and 5th Royal Green Jackets, with their headquarters still in Davies Street in London. The Light Infantry has a further four TA Battalions (5, 6, 7 and 8 LI) mainly recruited on a broadly regional basis which accounts for the disparity of numbers between the two Regiments comprising the Light Infantry Division.

Northern Ireland

Since the re-emergence of the troubles in Northern Ireland in the 60s, the Royal Green Jackets have played a very important role in maintaining order and rooting out IRA terrorists in what was at first an extraordinarily difficult and unusual role. All three Battalions of the Regiment have gained an outstanding reputation for their conduct of operations in the province. In the early period, at the beginning of the 70s, they were renowned for their active and aggressive patrolling while at the same time maintaining calm in the face of crisis. They have suffered a number of casualties since they became involved and the early 70s in particular took their toll of regular Royal Green Jacket riflemen.

In 1972, the 1st Battalion was deployed in the Andersontown area and had one man killed and 12 wounded as a result of terrorist action. The Battalion captured numerous weapons and explosives, searched 320 houses, arrested 170 people and claimed seven hits on gunmen, before returning to Germany after a four-month deployment. During this same early period of the 70s, the 2nd Battalion lost one officer and three other ranks with six seriously wounded and the 3rd Battalion suffered 3 fatalities and 22 other casualties while inflicting considerable loss on the IRA.

At no time since the formation of the early rifle regiments has the inherent quality of quick-thinking, positive action of The Royal Green Jackets been more severely and successfully tested than in Northern Ireland. Success is perhaps a difficult word to swallow in this continual war of attrition, especially considering the losses of men and the exceptional difficulty of pursuing military activity in urban areas where the greater majority of people are peace-loving individuals conducting their lives as they would anywhere else in the UK. Ulster has been a phenomenally trying experience for the Army in general with a continually precarious balance between military and political expedience making the work of any force helping the Royal Ulster Constabulary an operational tight-rope walking experience in the public eye. More recently, with the Northern Ireland problem so much the breach in the UK's otherwise reasonably equanamous image in the world's view, The Royal

Above: A typical rifle section plans tactics during a training exercise. In time of hostilities, RGJ Battalions would be divided between front-line duties with the BAOR, and home defence following a recent re-allocation of units.

Green Jackets have learnt to adopt even more softly softly approaches. These entail making their presence sufficiently felt to create a deterrent effect against IRA hostilities without in any way creating undue friction with the local population. Living in impromptu barracks and having little contact with the civilian population (as is normally far from being the situation in garrison towns in the UK) puts some strain on soldiers serving in these conditions. The Regiment has 20 years' experience of the peculiar problems of the province. It now trains its soldiers at Flowerdown Light depot near Winchester, and at Tidworth (home of the 1st Battalion) to recognise and cope with the vicissitudes of this temporary lifestyle as well as versing every recruit in the many military skills involved in anti-terrorist fighting.

The Falklands

The Falklands Conflict was not The Royal Green Jacket's claim to fame. Like many others they embarked and underwent the difficult sea journey only to arrive shortly after the hostilities had ended. The Battalion that was sent down nevertheless experienced the tensions created by the conflict when they arrived, and were on a Standby footing until they returned. The 1st Battalion has quite recently (the end of 1985) returned from a six-month unaccompanied tour of The Falklands where it took its turn in manning the garrison.

The Royal Green Jackets today

Speed over the ground, rapid and effective deployment of soldiers carrying light infantry weapons, daring and positive action all combine to form the raison d'etre of today's Royal Green Jackets just as they did at the time of the early Regiments. The principal difference in operational activity is the inevitable one of maximising the use of the increasingly mechanised units in BAOR teeth-arm Battle Groups. The modern infantry has to be very fast to keep up with the new Challenger tanks. The new Infantry Combat Vehicle – the Japanese-designed MCV 80 – is this year being introduced to replace the existing FV432 which seems clumsy by comparison.

Another quite recent development for The Royal Green Jackets is the adoption of a Home defence role. The 1st Battalion, based at Tidworth in Wiltshire, trains almost continually in the Home Defence role and has now been fully converted to be able to play its part in the protection of vital bases and ground installations. Air-mobility and minimum footwork are fundamental to this new role.

These are the prevailing new developments in The Royal Green Jackets with the relatively new Home defence role adding to their other main activities in Northern Ireland and BAOR. In Germany, the Battalions stay

for a tour of about two years at a time whereas in Northern Ireland the tours tend to be between four and five months on a 'roulement' basis – one Battalion taking over from another to maintain a continual presence in support of the RUC.

Despite the apparent routine of the three Battalions' movements between Germany, Northern Ireland and their base depots, The Royal Green Jackets are one of several frontline Regiments used for emergency tours that may be required at any time anywhere in the world. The following account of each of the Battalion's appointments illustrates the variety inherent in Royal Green Jacket life.

1st Battalion

Since the summer of 1985 the 1st Battalion have been in The Falklands, Kenya, Northern Ireland, Tidworth and West Germany. After a six-month tour in The Falklands which was unaccompanied and involved routine garrison defence and the protection of base camps and outposts as well as the new airport – to some extent a role matching the Battalion's new Home Defence activities – the Battalion returned to England in time to go to Kenya in early 1986. Training in Kenya is very different from the activities of The Falklands. The grassland and jungle terrain affords good firing range practice and plenty of scope for patrol exercises. Each of the two or three different regimental Battalions of the British Army which go there every year make maximum use of these training facilities.

On returning from Kenya in early March the Battalion got barely a fortnight's notice to go on an emergency tour for four months to Northern Ireland. This Royal Green Jacket Battalion was required to strengthen the British military presence in the context of politically important Anglo-Irish agreements which were likely to

cause IRA terrorist action. The two extra battalions sent out at the same time, including 1st Battalion, brought the total number of troops to more than 10,000 in Northern Ireland. Within four days of their arrival, the 1st Battalion suffered the first casualty of the year. Rifleman David Mulley, aged 20, was part of an eight-man patrol escorting an RUC officer on duty in Castlewellan, County Down, when a Provisional IRA bomb was detonated in a derelict pub. The explosion killed Rifleman Mulley and caused extensive damage to surrounding shops and houses. The Government sent an additional 550 troops to the province after this action.

In August 1986 1st Battalion returned from Northern Ireland to their base in Tidworth to continue training in their Home Defence role. Equipped with Fox Armoured Cars, Milan Anti-Tank ground weapons, 81 mm mortars, SLRs and the heavier fire capacity GPMG (SF), their training purpose is to pack a punch in rapid defence movements against potential insurgent forces. After their Tidworth training they left for Osnabrucke where they were based at the beginning of this year.

2nd Battalion

The 2nd Battalion were on a longer tour in West Germany based in Minden until July 1986 when they packed up and returned to England to take up a far more routine and often pleasantly predictable lifestyle as the Infantry Demonstration Battalion at Warminster in Wiltshire. Interrupting their Minden tour came a 4½ month tour in Northern Ireland joining up with the 1st Battalion in support of the RUC.

Life at Warminster for any operational British Battalion is in many ways mundane and quite relaxing compared to the exigencies of living in a converted school-house or mill in Northern Ireland, or honing and refining the complex battle procedures required of the Infantry Battalions in the frontline of the BAOR. Members of the Infantry Demonstration Battalions at Warminster are used as bodies on the ranges in that area, and demonstrate the use of new equipment, or tactical formations to visiting dignatories and NATO or other senior staff commanders. They work far more routine hours and take part in the countless practical courses designed to augment the skills of certain Army officers selected for promotion right up to the rank of Major General. To many of the soldiers involved weekend leave is a pleasant novelty.

The 2nd Battalion will spend two years in total at Warminster and get a new perspective on military life generally after having spent five (interrupted) years in West Germany.

3rd Battalion

For the best part of the last five years the 3rd Battalion has been based in Celle, West Germany as part of the 1st Armoured Division. It has operated in a mechanised role as an advanced battalion working closely with armoured units in combat teams making up part of the frontline Battle Groups. For this task the Battalion has been using the Sultan APC with a GPMG gun mounted

Below: Transport of the 3rd Battalion the Royal Green Jackets leaving Celle, West Germany, where the Battalion have largely been based until their recent move back to Colchester as part of 19 Reinforcement Brigade.

on top; Recce platoons of the mechanised Battalion travel in Scimitars carrying 81 mm mortars inside. The majority of the infantry are still using the rather slow and cumbersome FV432 APCs with the GPMG mounted gun equipment that is far too slow for the new mechanised infantry role in BAOR. Keeping up with Challenger tanks in rough terrain demands advanced equipment for the infantry involved in the combat teams. Although the Sultans are reasonably fast, they do not have the speed or versatility of the new MCV 80S which are being introduced this year. The MCV 80 has undergone extensive, very successful pre-production trials which have indicated that the Japanese have got their figures right in its design and engineering. The British Army in Germany are looking forward to this vehicle, mounted with a 35 mm Rarden Cannon which has terrific firepower making the new APC immensely valuable in the combat teams.

The 3rd Battalion has worked in its mechanised role either in an infantry heavy combat team, usually 2:1 infantry to armour, or an armour heavy team (the reverse ratio). This formation is intended to be flexible and there is a certain amount of pairing and swapping of roles within the Battle Group or Brigade, each of which has a certain number of allocated combat teams. The 3rd Battalion RGJ has been very much involved in the learning curve of the new mechanised Battalions in BAOR.

In the summer the 3rd Battalion returned to Colchester to become part of 19 Reinforcement Brigade and has been training in a reinforcement role since then.

Chapter 4

SEA WAR: PLASTIC NAVY

One of Britain's major commitments to NATO is to guarantee freedom of the Western Approaches to Alliance shipping in time of war. Consequently the Navy's mine counter-measures forces must continually probe these waterways for the many and various devices which lie on the seabed waiting to strike against unsuspecting supply vessels and warships that are vital to the reinforcement of NATO in Europe.

Royal Navy mine-hunters in the Channel.

When it was announced that the Royal Navy's new mine-hunters were to be made out of glass reinforced plastic (GRP), old-time matelots promptly dubbed them the "toy boats of Her Majesty's plastic navy." It was an unfair description which has since been disproved by the ships' handling qualities and ability to carry out the tasks for which they were designed. The truth is that only plastic ships can perform the exceedingly dangerous and sophisticated duty of hunting for modern mines fitted with all manner of devilish traps for the unwary. Small wonder, then, that this new class is named after fox hunts – risking the displeasure of the animals rights lobby – precisely because their quarry is so cunning and elusive.

Mine warfare at sea goes back to the American Civil War, the conflict which first harnessed science and industrial power to war. Mines did not become genuinely effective, however, until the Russo-Japanese war of 1904 when both sides used crude but highly effective contact mines. In just over a year's fighting the Japanese navy lost two battleships, four cruisers, two destroyers and a torpedo boat to Russian mines laid, not as harbour defences, but as offensive weapons on the high seas. At the same time the Russians lost a battleship, a cruiser, two destroyers, a torpedo boat and a gunboat to mines – although the battleship probably ran on to one of their own.

These losses convinced the major naval powers of the effectiveness of the mine and it was used extensively in both World Wars. Some 70,000 were laid by the British and American navies in the North Sea in 1918 in an attempt to prevent the Kaiser's U-Boats from breaking out into the North Atlantic to attack the convoys bringing fresh young American troops to the Western Front to support the worn-out Allied armies.

In World War II the Germans laid 100,000 mines which sank 650 ships while the Allies laid 250,000, sending over 1,000 German and Italian ships to the bottom. In the Far East the mine proved to be an even more devastating weapon, sinking more than 2 million tons of Japanese shipping. The effect of the mines was not only measured in terms of ships sunk but also in terms of men and ships diverted to countering them. By the end of the war the Allies had no less than 300,000 men serving on 1,500 minesweepers while the Germans had to assign over half their sailors to minesweeping duties.

Russians learn lessons of mining

It is surprising therefore that, despite this indisputable evidence of the cost-effectiveness of the mine as a weapon, the Western nations paid little attention to developing modern minesweepers after the end of the war. The Russians, who had never forgotten the lessons of 1904, made no such mistakes. They continued to develop their minesweepers and, especially, their intricate mines triggered by a number of different detonating devices.

Above: US Navy personnel await the order to launch a MK6 Model 5 Anchored Mine during exercises in Subic Bay, in the Philippines.

It was the war in Korea which brought Britain and the United States to their senses. One particular incident delivered the message: a fleet of 250 modern ships carrying an invasion force of 50,000 US Marines heading for Wonsan was held up for eight days by a minefield of 3,500 Russian-made contact and magnetic influence mines improbably laid by a fleet of North Korean junks and sampans. The commander of the invasion fleet, Rear Admiral A.E.Smith, shook his head disgustedly and said: "We have lost control of the sea to a nation without a Navy using obsolete weapons, delivered by ships which were in use at the time of Jesus Christ."

What particularly disturbed the western navies was that the old technique of "degaussing" ships had no effect on the Russian magnetic mines. Even worse, it was discovered that while the hulls of wooden ships would not set them off, the metal machinery in those hulls would. So the western navies had to completely rethink their approach to countering the threat of the mine.

This rethink led to the building of new classes of mine countermeasures vessels in the United States and Britain which were quite unlike the old minesweepers. They had wooden hulls and their machinery was designed to give a much lower "magnetic signature". The Americans produced the *Agile* (subseqently, *Agressive*) class while the Royal Navy turned out no less than 120 of the *Ton* class. These little ships displacing 425 tons with a length of 150 feet (46 metres), became well-loved in the navy, serving not only as anti-mine vessels but also as Fishery Protection ships while a number were sold to Hong Kong for patrol duties.

Enter the *Hunt* class

It was one of the *Tons*, HMS *Wilton* MIII6, which took the navy into the plastic era. She was built of GRP in

Above: USS *Pledge,* one of the new type of wooden-hulled minesweepers developed as a result of the Korean War experience, seen underway off Point Loma, San Diego.

Above: HMS *Wilton,* the first of the *Ton* class glass reinforced plastic (GRP) coastal minesweeper/minehunters built for the Royal Navy.

order to test the material in day-to-day use. Meanwhile work started on a new generation of plastic MCM vessels capable of undertaking a variety of minesweeping and minehunting duties.

Every effort was made in the design of these vessels to reduce their magnetic signatures to the lowest possible level to defeat magnetic detonators and to cut their underwater noise to defeat acoustic detonators. At the same time they were required to maintain the ability to make deep-sea journeys to any part of the world.

It was these ships which became the *Hunt* class, the first of which, HMS *Brecon*, was built by Vosper Thorneycroft and came into service in 1979. With a standard displacement of 615 tons, a length of 200 feet (60 metres) and a beam of 32 feet (10 metres), they are the largest GRP-hulled ships in the world. And at £35 million each they are the most expensive. At the time of writing eight are operational, another three are building, and several more are planned.

They are officially designated minehunter/sweeper coastal (MHSC) and there is a school of thought in the navy that it would be cheaper and more efficient to have "one class, one role" vessels, a view reflected in the next class of GRP hulled "single role" MCMVs now on order. The argument in favour of the "single role" vessels is that as they are smaller and simpler many more of them can be built for the money it takes to produce a few *Hunts*.

In the *Hunts'* favour is the fact that because it has been designed for a multiplicity of roles it has the endurance and the equipment to deal with almost any situation in any part of the world. HMS *Brecon* and her sister ship HMS *Ledbury* have, for example, cleared Argentinian mines from the Falkland waters.

It is necessary at this point to discuss the sort of mine the Hunts are designed to combat, either by hunting or sweeping. Mines can be laid with one of two objects in mind: defensive or offensive. In the defensive role they are laid in 'fields' to protect ports and convoy routes and to close off certain areas to enemy ships. In the offensive role they are laid to sink enemy ships and prevent the use of harbours and waterways. These offensive mines can be laid by ship, submarine or aircraft. Oneol increasingly worrying prospect is that mines might be laid clandestinely by merchant ships either immediately before the outbreak of hostilities or, with a 'sleeping' detonator, to be called into action once hostilities have started.

Libyans foil Russians

The Libyans are believed to have 'blown the gaff' on Russian plans in this respect by spreading mines

Left: Royal Navy divers undertake a number of roles and missions as part of their duties. These can include obstacle clearance in both home ports and during naval assault operations in enemy-controlled waters. They also conduct underwater searches of naval vessels for enemy-planted magnetic mines.

Above: HMS *Brecon*, the first of the Navy's *Hunt* Class vessels is the largest plastic-hulled minesweeper in the World. She fulfils the dual role of both minehunter and minesweeper.

through the Red Sea from the roll-on roll-off ferry, *Ghat*, while it was making a seemingly innocuous return trip between the Suez Canal and Ethiopia in July 1984. The mines damaged 19 ships in what was apparently a wild-cat terrorist operation by the Libyans to frighten ships into boycotting the Suez Canal. Strangely none of the ships was sunk. It is believed that this was because most of the mines did not carry a full charge of explosive.

This was not the case with the example recovered by divers from HMS *Gavinton*, one of the *Ton* class, which took part in a multi-nation sweep to clear the Red Sea. In a classic exercise in mine-hunting for which Fleet Chief Petty Officer (Diver) Terence Settle was awarded the Queen's Gallantry Medal, the mine was recovered from within a defensive Egyptian minefield and discovered to be fully loaded with 1650 lbs (750 kg) of high explosive. This was eventually steamed out using a boiler flown from Britain with two Royal Engineers to operate it. But before they could get to work, FCPO Settle had to disarm the brute. And he made some alarming discoveries. He found that it could be set off in three ways: magnetic impulses from a ship's hull, noise from its propellors or machinery, or the reduction in water pressure caused by the passage of the ship.

It had to be handled with extreme care. In order to foil the magnetic and acoustic detonators Settle used non-magnetic tools which he had to be careful not to drop. The rewards of his expertise were great. Not only did the West get a glimpse of the way the Soviet Union plans to use 'neutral' merchant ships but also gleaned a wealth of information about the technology of the Russians' new mines.

Known Soviet mine types

Like most states with a modern navy the Russians have a number of types of mine. The most familiar is the old fashioned moored mine which can be cleared by vessels towing wire sweeps to cut the mines' mooring wires allowing them to rise to the surface where they are dealt with by small-arms fire. There is, however a modern version of the moored mine which is much more difficult to clear. Laid in deep water, it can sense when a ship is approaching and release a warhead which homes on the sound of the ship's propellors. To deal with this development the Royal Navy has invented a deep running sweep called the Extra Deep Armed Trawler Sweep (EDATS).

Then there are the magnetic and acoustic mines which lie in wait for their prey on the sea-bed. These are dealt with by specially designed ships, like the *Hunts,* with low noise and magnetic profiles, which explode them by towing underwater noise-makers or creating a strong magnetic field by sending a heavy current through a towed double wire.

Mines quite often have both magnetic and acoustic detonators. What made the Red Sea mine so interesting was that it also had a pressure detonator, a triple combination previously thought too dangerous to put together.

Pressure mines are quite difficult enough to clear on their own. They are sea-bed mines and cannot be swept. They have to be hunted individually, picked out by sonar and then tracked down by teams of divers or remotely controlled mini-subs.

There are other nasties too, which make the mine hunters' task exceedingly difficult, like the mine which burrows into the sea-bed to avoid detection, or the version which moves around the sea-bed under its own power.

Hunts designed to deal with variety of problems

Against these enemies, the Hunts pit their design, their crews and their equipment. The design, as we have seen, gives the vessel as much protection as possible from acoustic and magnetic mines. All the machinery operates on sound-absorbing, resilient mountings and when it is actually hunting, propellor noise is reduced to a minimum, barely ticking over at three to four knots.

The hull itself has no magnetic signature and everything possible on board, even the ship's safe, is made from non-metallic material. Machinery which necessarily contains ferrous material, such as the engines, carries individual 'degaussing' equipment, while items such as cables and tools are made of non-magnetic phosphor-bronze. The disadvantage of this is that being soft, the phosphor-bronze tends to wear out quickly.

Another problem encountered is that with the hull being completely non-magnetic, the ship's own electronic systems get no shielding from other vessels' electronics radiations. Special screening has had to be devised to protect the systems from interference. However the need to present a minimal magnetic signature is so important that this is a small price to pay. Even the ship's 40 mm Bofors gun will be left behind if the *Hunts* go to war because of its magnetic influence. Surely this must be the first example of a warship disarming to do battle?

The crews, like all Royal Navy crews these days, are specialists, trained to operate the most complex equipment as well as – what is sometimes forgotten – remaining good seamen. Among the most highly trained are the divers who, when a contact is picked up by sonar, have to go down, often in rough water and zero visibility to identify the target and either recover it – a highly dangerous business – or destroy it with an explosive charge.

Unmanned submersible

The *Hunts* have another, mechanical system, for doing this job, the French built PAP 104 unmanned wire-guided submersible which is launched from the ship and guided along a sonar beam to its target. Its batteries are good for an hour and a half and it has enough wire to travel up to 3000 feet (1000 metres) from the mother ship. It carries a searchlight and a closed circuit TV camera which relays its film back to the Operations Room. The target can thus be positively identified. If the decision is taken to destroy the target orders will be relayed to the mini-sub to 'lay its egg' – drop an explosive charge next to the mine. Then, when it has been recovered and the mother ship moved to a safe distance the charge and the target will be detonated by an ultrasonic signal.

The mini-sub is only one of the *Hunt's* devices. It has one for every occasion. There is the Sperry Osborn TAG acoustic system, a cylindrical generator towed behind the ship which imitates the noise not only of a ship's propellor but also of its machinery. The plot is for the quiet *Hunt* to pass safely over the mine which picks up and 'destroys' the TAG.

It also carries the MM Mark II magnetic loop system which again is towed behind the ship and is fed with current from an auxiliary engine to set off magnetic mines at a safe distance from the non-magnetic *Hunts*. Then, to deal with old-fashioned moored contact mines, it carries an Oropesa wire sweep which has been in use for about as long as the moored mine.

Controlling all this activity is the Computer Assisted Action Information System (CAAIS) which is linked to the Type 193 Sonar and projects information about all the systems onto a screen in the Ops Room.

Reports speak well of the Hunts despite some initial problems with their revolutionary technology. It was thought at first that the GRP would be a fire hazard. In fact the reverse seems to be the case for woven cloth is used to reinforce the glass fibre and when the resin in the GRP burns the woven cloth acts as a fire blanket. The plastic construction of the hull has also proved extremely easy to repair. It does not rust like steel, neither does it rot like wood. And marine growths and boring worms hate it. Maintenance is cheap and simple to carry out and the hulls have a life expectancy of 60 years.

A maintenance unit given the designation of FSO 01 has been formed especially to care for the *Hunts*. It is made up of 16 ordinary freight containers which hold everything the *Hunts* might need and include workshops and living quarters. It has its own generators and, when it needs to move to look after its vessels, it simply loads the containers onto its own articulated lorries and drives off.

New class to benefit from hindsight

The lessons learnt in the *Hunts* are reflected in the design of the new Single Role Mine Hunter (SRMH). The first order for this class, as yet unnamed, was placed with Vosper Thorneycroft in 1985. The aim, according to Mr John Lee, the Under Secretary of State for Defence Procurement, is to build a "low cost, highly efficient ship taking full advantage of the latest technology."

Only 160 feet (50 metres) long and 30 feet(9 metres) wide, it will obviously not be able to carry the wide variety of 'kit' packed into the multi-role *Hunts*. Its job will be to do what its name suggests: it will hunt individual mines. It will have a complement of seven officers and 33 ratings and will be equipped with variable depth sonar to pick up deep-laid mines and a 'mine disposal system.'

This system seems likely to be based on a yet to be developed Remotely Operated Vehicle (ROV) which will in fact involve two vehicles being operated from one ship. The first will be a Remote Control Inspection Vehicle (RCIV) which will be a high speed mini-sub equipped with sonar and television cameras to hunt down and identify suspicious objects detected by the mother ship. Once it has made its identification, its partner, the Internally Controlled Mine Destruction System (ICMDS) will go into action, carrying a 200 lb (90 kg) charge to destroy the mine. There have been some eyebrows raised about the size of the demolition charge. It is thought to be unnecessarily large for the job and that its explosion would effect the delicate

Above: A PAP 104 Submersible being lowered into the water from a French *Circe*-Class Mine Counter-measures Vessel. It is used to detect and neutralize enemy seabed mines. Below: The TAG Towed Acoustic Generator on the afterdeck of a *Hunt*-Class vessel, designed to simulate the sound of a passing ship and so detonate a mine.

mechanism of the mine hunter's sonar.

Obviously the SRMH, a small vessel, necessarily filled with equipment, will not be over-generously provided with fuel, water and food. But as it must be capable of hunting mines anywhere along the Continental Shelf it will have to be able to be revictualled and refuelled at sea. It promises to be an interesting type of ship in which to serve.

River class based on oilrig supply ships

The third arm of Britian's mine counter measures force will be the new *River* class, of which several vessels are already serving. This sturdy, 900 ton, vessel is based on a North Sea oilrig supply ship design. Its role is that of fleet minesweeper and its function is to sweep the Soviet deep water mines which will be laid off the Scottish coasts in time of war to destroy British and American submarines on their way to their war stations. It is armed with the EDATS gear with which two vessels work together towing a deep running cable laced with explosive charges to help the mechanical cutters break the cables of moored mines.

Surface vessels are relatively safe from these deep-laid anti-submarine mines and so the *Rivers,* not need-ing a low magnetic signature, are being made of steel. As they come into service they are replacing the veteran *Ton* sweepers manned by the Royal Naval Reserve.

Despite the advent of these new ships, NATO's minesweeping forces remain woefully inadequate for any major conflict. For reasons of numbers as well as displaying solidarity NATO has formed the Standing Naval Force Channel, clumsily known as STANAVFORCHAN, which consists of six ships from Britain, Belgium, Holland and West Germany. GRP is incorporated in the design of all these MCMVs and plastic has now been accepted by most navies as the best material for building their mine hunters. This is how they do it:

The Belgian, French and Dutch navies have produced a joint design, the Tripartite Minesweeper, which has its hull, decks and partitions made out of GRP. Displacing 510 tons standard, these vessels, named the *Aster* class by Belgium, the *Eridan* by France and the *Alkmaar* by the Netherlands, carry minehunting sonar

HMS *Spey,* one of the new *River* Class mineswepers constructed from a design adapted from a North Sea oilrig supply ship, is specially built to tackle deep-water anti-submarine devices which are less sensitive to surface shipping.

Top: *Harlingen Alkmaar* Class Minehunter of the Royal Netherlands Navy, built to the Tripartite design agreed between France, Belgium and the Netherlands. Above left: *Circe,* a *Circe*-Class Minehunter of the French Navy, first introduced in the mid-1970s. Right: French Minehunter *Eridan,* the first of France's tripartite-built vessels.

and the PAP 104 mine-disposal system similar to that carried by the *Hunts*. Like most mine hunters they have auxiliary 'active rudder' systems for precise manoeuvring while tracking a mine.

The French also have their own *Circe* class of minehunters whose hulls are built of a wood and foam sandwich with the outer skin being covered by a thin film of GRP. The deckhead and the superstructure are made of a composite of glassfibre resin and wood. They are equipped with the DUBM 20 minehunting sonar, carry a team of six divers and the ubiquitous PAP 104.

They use the 'active rudder' system and all the prop-

ulsion systems can be worked either from the bridge or a specially sound-proofed control room.

German 'drones'

The Germans have introduced an interesting concept with their Lindau Type 351 class. These vessels, of 388 tons standard displacement, are made of wood laminated with plastic. The engines and the superstructure are made of non-magnetic materials. What makes these vessels so interesting is that they have been converted to operate a 'Troika', three remotely controlled 'Seehunde' minesweeping drones.

River Class minesweeper

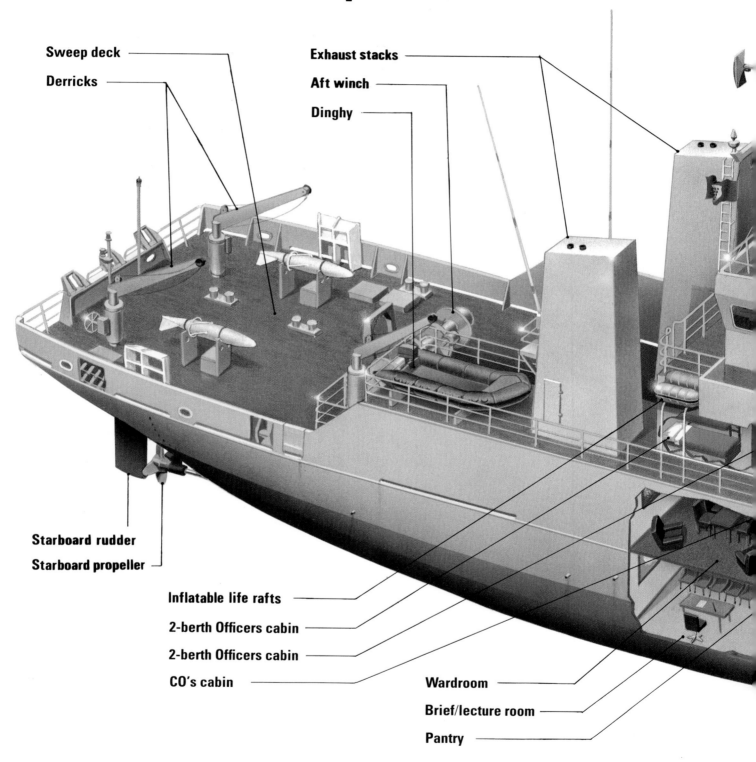

Sweep deck

Derricks

Exhaust stacks

Aft winch

Dinghy

Starboard rudder

Starboard propeller

Inflatable life rafts

2-berth Officers cabin

2-berth Officers cabin

CO's cabin

Wardroom

Brief/lecture room

Pantry

River Class minesweeper, the latest addition to the navy's mine countermeasures force, are specifically tasked to sweep enemy deep-water mines off the Scottish coast. Safe from these anti-submarine munitions, the type is built of steel.

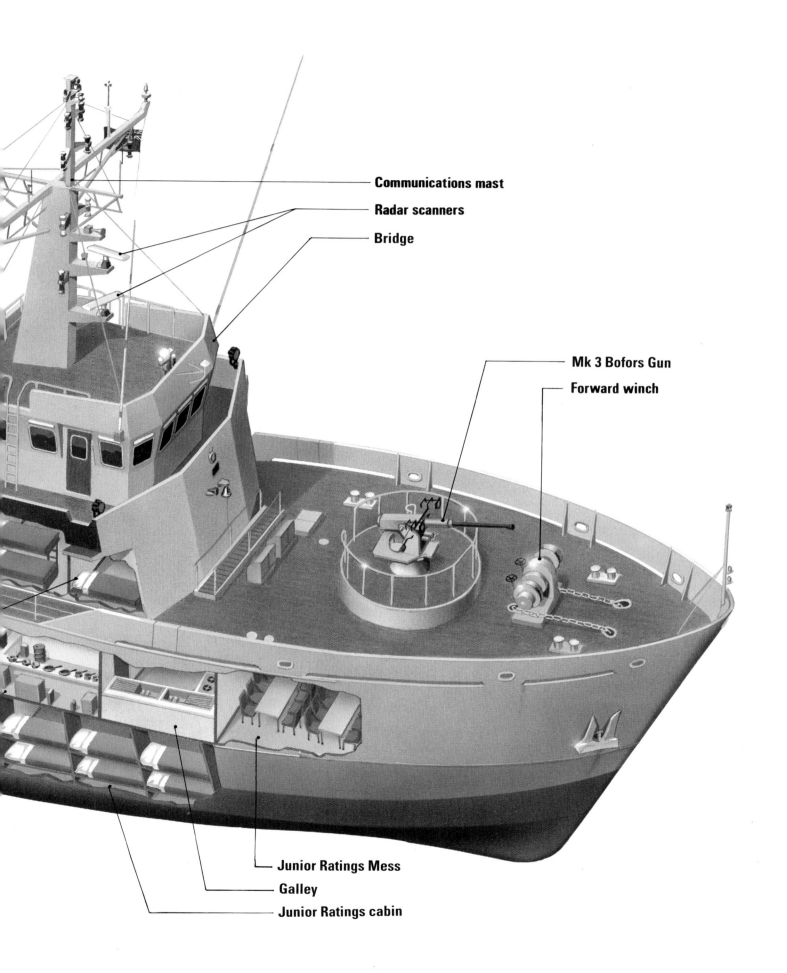

Communications mast

Radar scanners

Bridge

Mk 3 Bofors Gun

Forward winch

Junior Ratings Mess

Galley

Junior Ratings cabin

These small craft have a crew of three who are taken off when the mother ship assumes control. The drones are equipped to sweep for magnetic and acoustic mines and they are operated in a vee formation, spread out well in front of the mother ship which is thus protected from any exploding mines. If one of the drones is sunk, that is just too bad. Nobody gets hurt. The Germans are also planning new MCM vessels built out of GRP to come into service in the late 1980s and early 1990s.

The Italians are building boats of the *Lerici* class with GRP. Handsome, like most Italian craft, the *Lericis* follow customary MCMV techniques of low acoustic and magnetic signatures. Where they differ from other European types is in having an Italian built submersible instead of the French PAP 104.

Designated MIN-79, the mini-sub is fitted with a sonar and a TV system. It destroys ground mines in the usual way by laying an explosive charge alongside which is then remotely detonated. But it can also cut the cables of moored mines with small explosive charges. Four *Lericis* are in service and a further six of an improved design will be built when the money is available.

Australian catamarans

The Australians have entered the 'plastic navy' business with a most unusual design. Their MHCAT class of inshore minehunters are plastic catamarans. They are made of a Swedish-designed plastic sandwich consisting of layers of 2.5in (60mm) thick rigid PVC between ½in (8mm) thick skins of GRP. Two 1in (30mm) slabs of PVC being surfaced-glued to give the required 2.5in (60mm) thickness. With a length of 100 feet (31 metres) and a displacement of 100 tons standard, the MHCAT has a crew of 12. The catamaran layout gives the vessel

Above: HMAS *Rushcutter,* showing the foam sandwich hull with outer GRP lamination completed. Below: Impression of Swedish-designed catamaran Minehunter *Rushcutter* of the Australian Navy, due to enter Service in 1986.

stability and also enables the machinery to be positioned well above the waterline thus further reducing the magnetic and acoustic signatures. As much of its equipment as possible is supplied in packaged units, even the meals being 'pre-prepared'. It carries a DSQS-11H mine hunting sonar and the PAP 104 mine disposal system as well as a conventional sweep. The first prototype was due to put to sea in February 1986.

The Swedish plastic sandwich developed by the Karlskronavarvet company is enjoying considerable success. Apart from the Australians, it is being used by the Danish and United States navies for their MCMVs. The Swedes have also used the sandwich in designing their Landsort MCMV class which is up for sale around the world.

According to the advertisements it is: "Equipped with an integrated navigation and information system. Accurate positioning is achieved by a propulsion system with Voith-Schneider vertical propellors. The Landsort can carry any type of Mine Disposal Vehicle and all types of minesweeps." It is extraordinary that, given the current upsurge in the development of new types of GRP minehunters, the United States is lagging so far behind.

US falls behind in minesweeper technology

The first of a new class, the *Avenger*, is due to be commissioned in 1986, but because Congress has slashed the military budget only fourteen of these vessels will now be built, a total which will hardly dent the Soviets' ability to wage mine warfare. The *Avenger's* hull is built of laminated oak, fir and cedar wood and its superstructure is made of wood covered with GRP – not so much to provide a low magnetic imprint but to protect the wood from sea water. They are large vessels, 224 feet (68.3) metres long and displacing 1040 tons standard. They have a crew of 72, carry acoustic, magnetic and normal wire sweeps and are equipped with a minehunting SQQ-30 sonar which works with a Honeywell remote-controlled mini-sub Mine Neutralisation System.

The *Avengers* will be backed up by true GRP vessels, MSH-1 *Cardinal* class of small minehunters. Congress is being asked to approve funds for 17 of these vessels.

Most American mine counter measures have, however, been concentrated on helicopters using Sikorsky RH-53D Sea Stallions formed in Helicopter Mine Countermeasures Squadrons. They argue the 'choppers' can do almost anything ships can do at far less cost. It was Sea Stallions that swept Haiphong harbour clear of American mines when the United States pulled out of the Vietnam war. Less happily, eight of No

Above right: In the US, helicopters are widely used in the minehunting role, towing mine detonation systems. The Sikorsky MH-53E Super Stallion with enlarged fuel sponsons has been specially developed for these tasks. Below left: It tows a hydrofoil sledge through the water to detect and detonate enemy mines.

16 Squadron's Sea Stallions were commandeered for the abortive attempt to free American diplomatic hostages from Teheran. Only one came back.

Three main types of mine clearing equipment have been developed for use by the Sea Stallions. The first is a towed sweep equipped with cutters to sever the cables of moored mines. The clever aspect of this gear is that it can be transferred from one helicopter to another in midair.

The second is a towed noise-making device which simulates the sound of a ship passing through the water and so deceives acoustic mines into detonating harmlessly. The third is a Hydrofoil Platform which looks something like a sledge with retractable hydrofoils. This platform carries a generator that pumps current through two electrodes lowered into the water by a retractable boom. Towed some 450 feet behind the helicopter, this device creates a magnetic field similar to that of a ship and induces magnetic mines to explode without harming either the helicopter or the platform.

In a further example of technical skill, the Americans have mounted their noise maker on the magnetic sledge to form a combined sweep which will explode both acoustic and magnetic mines. To increase the endurance of the generator on the sledge, the helicopter can pump fuel to it through the towing cable. And the Sea Stallions themselves with a range of 257 miles at cruising speed can be refuelled in the air. However, there are not very many of these custom-built mine sweeping helicopters – a production run of 30 started in October 1972. And what happens if the weather is too bad for them to operate or their mother ship is sunk?

Russia – as advanced in sweepers as in mines?

At first sight the Russians would seem to be even further behind in the mine sweeping stakes than the Americans. As long ago as the 60s they experimented with three GRP-hulled prototypes of the *Zhenya* class. But they were not a success, apparently because the Russians did not have the technical ability to produce such large boats in plastic. While it is impossible to know what is going on in Russian dockyards, there is no sign that they have returned to GRP.

The most they have done is to coat the wooden hulls of their *Sonya* class minesweepers with fibreglass. It is thought that as with the American's *Avenger* this is less to do with magnetic signatures and more to do with wind, weather and marine organisms. The *Sonyas*, de-

Below: The West German Navy's Troika Minesweeping system incorporates remotely controlled sweep ships which precede the control vessel, and can sweep both magnetic and acoustic mines.

Above: A Soviet Navy *T 58* Class Ocean Minesweeper in the Atlantic Ocean. Although technologically inferior to Western counterparts, they are more numerous by far.

veloped from the failed *Zhenya* prototypes, are regarded as being the Soviet equivalent of the *Hunts*. There are about 50 vessels of this class in service with the Red Navy and others have been given or sold to various Eastern Bloc countries and Cuba.

The equipment carried by the *Sonyas* is crude by Western standards. They appear to rely on basic sweeps for dealing with moored, acoustic and magnetic mines and while they have minehunting sonar there is no indication that they are fitted with mini-subs. Like all Russian minesweepers they carry a much heavier fit of armaments than Western MCMVs. They have anti-aircraft SAM 4 missiles as well as twin 30mm and twin 25 mm turrets. Other types, such as the *Natya* ocean-going class, also carry two five-barrel RBU 1200 anti-submarine rock launchers.

Soviets copy German drones

The Red Navy is known to have experimented with a mine sweeping drone system similar to the West German 'Troika'. The Russians use a development of their *Vanya* class 200 ton standard minesweeper as mother ships controlling up to three Ilyusha drones. The Ilyushas are quite big craft, displacing some 85 tons when loaded and needing a crew of ten to work them before they come under control of the *Vanyas*.

Where the Soviet Union has a distinct advantage over the West is in the number of minesweeping and hunting vessels it has on the water. Although they may be steel-hulled, vulnerable and unsophisticated there are at least 200 of them of various classes.

They can therefore accept casualties which would cripple the West's defences against Soviet mines which, unlike their minesweepers, are becoming more and more sophisticated and more and more dangerous.

So the scientific battle of the mines goes on, with the West seeking technical answers to the Russian numbers – it is estimated they have a stock of half a million mines. What is surprising is that hydrofoils and hovercraft are at present playing no part in this battle.

At one stage it seemed possible that the Royal navy would adopt the hovercraft for mine sweeping. The BH7 Mk II craft, P235, was equipped with a full set of minehunting sonar and navigation systems and used throughout 1983 in a series of trials. It was thought that the hovercraft's low underwater signature and its relative immunity to underwater explosions would make it ideal for mine hunting. But nothing concrete seems to have emerged from the trials.

There might, however be hope for the hovercraft in the United States where two 100 ton test craft have undergone trials with a possible production order for as many as 140. The roles for which they are being considered are missile firing, anti-submarine warfare and mine counter measures.

In the meantime, the 'Plastic Navy' is forming the front line of the West's defences against the threat of mine warfare and the *Hunt* class seems likely to play a leading part for many years to come.

Chapter 5

FORCES LIFE: DAD'S ARMIES?

Certainly not! – is the short answer. With an increasing reliance on the Territorial and Auxiliary forces following defence budget cuts, all three Services are finding a valuable fund of committed, skilled – and inexpensive – manpower resources among the country's growing part-time soldiery.

Part-time soldiery offers many a welcome break from routine.

The concept of nationally organised regular armed forces is fairly modern. Long before there was a regular army, local volunteer forces were used to defend the realm, rallying around the banners of their local aristocracy, and temporarily abandoning their civilian occupations to fight as infantry, cavalry, archers and pikemen. When the battles were over they returned to their villages and towns, becoming once again farmers, labourers and tradesmen. The modern auxiliary services are the inheritors of that tradition. There is a particular attraction for a large number of men and women all over the country in donning uniform, submitting to service training and discipline, and preparing for war, for at least part of the year. The motivations of these volunteers are many and various, ranging from a restlessness with the 'pub and telly' recreations of civilian life, to a passionate desire to express their patriotism in active fashion.

This is no mere 'playing at soldiers'. Apart from anything else the voluntary services, now more than at any other time, form a large and essential part of the country's mobilisable defences. Their role, on land, at sea, and in the air, is in the process of a major expansion.

Auxiliary services to expand

With a working deadline of 1990, the then Minister of Defence, Michael Heseltine, announced in March 1984 a radical increase in the numbers and re-equipment of all the country's auxiliary services. The largest by far of these services is the Territorial Army, which echoes the regular army with its regimental structure and the range of its functions. Under the TA umbrella also comes the Home Service Force, for the defence of strategically important installations in time of war. The naval equivalent of the TA is the Royal Naval Reserve, which specialises in mine-sweeping, and has its own vessels. The Royal Naval Auxiliary Service (RNXS) has units all around the British coast, and supports the Royal Navy locally, particularly in the tasks of naval control of merchant shipping (NCS) and the defence of ports and anchorages (DEFPA). The Royal Marines Reserve (RMR) performs similar tasks to the regular RM. The Royal Maritime Auxiliary Service (RMAS) consists of civilians working in support roles to the Royal Navy such as tug operation, pilotage in Admiralty waters, victualling, and ammunition organisation. The Royal Auxiliary Airforce (RAuxAF) provides ground defence forces for front-line RAF airfields, intelligence and communications personnel to back up the RAF in the three joint Naval/Air Maritime Headquarters, aeromedical evacuation services, and movements services for regular RAF tasks. Other auxiliary services include the Royal Observer Corps, which is under the direction of the Home Office. The Ulster Defence Regiment contains volun-

Below: US Air Force Police join forces with British Territorials under simulated attack on an airbase in Britain during the Brave Defender exercise in 1985. Such installations would be prime targets for advance units.

teer members from civilian life, who work alongside the full-timers of the Permanent Cadre.

There are a number of reasons for the decision to expand the volunteer services. The changing nature of warfare has something to do with it. As hi-tech weaponry, communications, and other defence systems become ever more complex, the full-time regular serviceman and servicewoman is forced increasingly into specialisations. Training becomes longer, more technical, and more expensive. The myriad general jobs expected of service personnel in the past, from guard duty to medical support, are increasingly difficult to fit in with the specialist tasks. It makes sense to train volunteers for the more general tasks, leaving the regulars to get on with their specialisations.

Nato commitment of regulars

Another good reason for a volunteer force is highlighted by the demands made on the regular forces by NATO requirements. A very large proportion of the regular force is committed to tasks outside of the UK in the event of war. This would leave a dangerously unmanned Britain if it were not for volunteer services. Even so, a great percentage of the infantry of 1 British Corps, the army's main German fighting force, is composed of TA

Below: The last decade has seen a remarkable integration of the Territorial and Auxiliary bodies into the overall fighting capability of the regular armed forces. They now receive specialist equipment – not just hand-me-downs.

– over 50%. The TA supplies 85% of 1 British Force's medical support. Anything that stretches the resources of the regular services increases the need for auxiliary forces, and a further reason for the current expansion of auxiliaries could well be the growing difficulty of the regulars in holding on to personnel, especially officers and senior NCOs. Many of these men and women are going on to civilian jobs after finishing their first engagements, rather than signing on again. The commitment of the volunteers is seen as more dependable in many cases than that of regulars whose motivations may be mainly mercenary.

But perhaps the most powerful reasons for expanding the auxiliary forces are economic. There is no getting away from the fact that the auxiliaries are an exceptional bargain. Britain's defence expenditure is the highest in Europe both as a total amount, and on a per capita basis. Within NATO it is second only to the USA in defence spending, and is far less able to afford its major contribution. The greater the role of the volunteers, the more able is Britain to afford its NATO commitments. Members of the various auxiliary services are paid a rate close to that of their regular counterparts, but for far less time, and without any of the regular running costs such as accommodation, food etc. For example, while a regular soldier costs somewhere in the region of £11,900 each year, his TA equivalent only costs about £2,540. In 1984, the TA cost a total of £220 million, 4.4 percent of the Army's total budget, and 1.4 percent of

total defence spending. For a force that represents a substantial one quarter to one third of the Army's mobilized strength, that is a bargain indeed. The same is true of the other auxiliary services. The Royal Naval Auxiliary Service is a special bargain, as its members are unpaid. For a very low outlay that must be the envy of every other NATO member, Britain benefits from the services of a dedicated and enthusiastic body of men and women, whose training and professionalism match that of the regular services.

The Territorial Army

Prior to 1967 the TA was a large-scale force of volunteers with a modest level of training and, in peacetime, no great sense of urgency. It was very much the poor relation of the regular army, with outdated, hand-me-down equipment. In the event of an emergency the TA's role was to come to action-readiness over several weeks of preparation. That all changed in 1967 when it was decided to reduce numbers by at least 50 percent to under 50,000, who were to be trained up to the point where they could be instantly ready for action if an emergency was declared. The deadline for the new, slimmer, fitter TA was 1970. Thus in 1967 the Territorial Army and the Army Emergency Reserve were combined to become the Territorial and Auxiliary Volunteer Reserve. In 1979 the title reverted to Territorial Army. By this time the TA had been divided into two groups, A and B. Group A, which includes the majority of TA personnel, has higher training and call-out obligations than group B. Most group A units are what is known as Independent Units, which are locally recruited, based on permanent TA centres, with permanent staff, and much of their own equipment. Sponsored Units consist of technical and other specialists who are recruited country-wide, not having their own centres. They are administered by Central Volunteer Headquarters of the parent Corps. Members of Sponsored Units have civilian skills which can be employed directly, not needing a lengthy army training. For this reason, the attendance requirement is lower than in the Independent Units, and consists of an annual 15 day camp, plus another 4 days.

Group B also consists of both Sponsored and Independent Units. Most members come from University Officer's Training Corps – there are 19 of these throughout the country. Until April 1986 the 22 TA bands were in Group B, with home defence duties in time of mobilisation. After that date they were transferred to Group A, with a war role as medical auxiliaries in 1 British Corps.

Group C is a category of its own, and consists of the Home Service Force. This completely new organisation was set up in 1982 for a trial run. The aim was to produce a force of men with service experience who could take over the defence of vital installations in war-time within the UK. This would release regular and other TA personnel for more active tasks. The Home Service Force certainly caters for older men who might not wish

Above: Members of the Home Service Force defending a key point in the UK. These units will release others to reinforce Europe.

to put in the same training commitment as the TA Independent Units, though it would be unwise to breathe the words 'Dad's Army' within hearing of a Home Services Force member. They come from the regular services, other auxiliary services, cadet force officers and instructors, and the Ministry of Defence police. They can enlist up to 50 years of age, though there is a minimum age of 20, and they continue to serve until their sixtieth birthdays if they wish. The initial commitment is a minimum of three years service for all ranks.

The pilot scheme which started in 1982 with four HSF companies was extremely successful. Units were recruited locally and assigned to Key Points (KPs) which they would defend in time of war. Technically the HSF can be called out by Royal order in time of emergency under what is known as the Lower Liability. Most TA units called out under this authority would be liable to serve anywhere in the world, but the HSF would be limited to the UK, the Channel Islands and the Isle of Man.

HSF pilot a success

Following on the success of the pilot scheme, the HSF, which currently numbers 2,800 has become subject to the general expansion of auxiliaries. By 1990 the original 4 companies will have become 47, and total strength will be close to 5,000. HSF volunteers, all with at least two years satisfactory service on their previous service units, must carry out a minimum of ten days training a year. This is usually done at weekends, with a voluntary training evening once a month. They are equipped with standard combat gear, and armed, where necessary, with rifles and light machine guns. The HSF units are 'hosted' by both TA and regular units, and will eventually all be 'badged', that is, assigned to specific regiments, whose badges they will wear as part of their uniform.

The first phase of the TA expansion ran from 1982 to the end of 1985, with the main aim of improving the ex-

isting establishments. £17 million was spent in capital costs. Recruiting and permanent staffing were improved, and increases made in Infantry numbers, medical support, and the reconnaissance function of the Yeomanry regiments, among other changes. Phase 2, which began in 1986, is a much more ambitious expansion, with a planned capital budget of £136 million. By 1990 the TA's current strength of about 76,500 should have reached a target strength of 86,000. A large part of the increase in numbers will be accounted for by the creation of six new Infantry Battalions. These are:
1st Battalion Yorkshire and Cleveland Volunteers,
8th Battalion the Light Infantry (Volunteers),
3rd (Volunteer) Battalion, The Cheshire Regiment,
5th (Volunteer) Battalion The Royal Green Jackets,
8th (Volunteer) Battalion The Queen's Fusiliers,
3rd Battalion The Devon and Cornwall Rifle Volunteers.

Major Hugh Babbington-Smith is the regular army officer in charge of setting up the 5th (Volunteer) Battalion The Royal Green Jackets, which is to be based at Oxford. He explained the staffing structure of a TA battalion.

"In a TA battalion you've got three kinds of staff – the regular staff, the non-regular permanent staff or NRPS, and then you've got the Territorials themselves. Regular personnel are on career postings with the TA. For instance, I'm a major, and my career posting is training major, which is a senior major's job with a TA Battalion for two years. I'll do two years, and then I'll go, and may never come back to the TA again. In each company you get two Permanent Staff Instructors, the training PSI who's a sergeant major, and a quartermaster PSI, who's a permanent man who looks after stores. They too are regular men on career postings of two years. In Battalion Headquarters you have the Commanding Officer. Roughly speaking a battalion will have alternate TA and regular COs, though that isn't a hard and fast rule. There's a training major – myself – and an adjutant, who is always a regular on a two year posting.

There are one or two others, and it amounts to roughly a dozen regular staff on the staff of a TA battalion. They're assisted by about a dozen non-regular permanent staff. Each company will have a NRPS Captain, who is the permanent staff Administrative Officer. He's usually a soldier who has come up through the ranks to be perhaps commissioned as a quarter-master, or retired as a warrant officer. He has Captain status, and is on the strength of the TA company. He can't be posted anywhere else. That's his job, for ten or fifteen years or whatever. He has no mobilisation role. He's simply there to be the man on the ground at all times, and to run the company administratively. Invariably the NRPS have been regular army.

There are others, such as the MT Colour-Sergeant.

Right: Members of the Home Service Force must have served a minimum of 2 years in the armed forces and provide a body of considerable military experience. Their equipment is similar to that issued to other Territorial and Auxiliary units.

Their great advantage is that they are always there. There's a lot to be done behind the scenes so that things will be ready for the territorials when they come in. The volunteers are working frantically when they are in, but outside they don't think about the TA, by and large. Out of sight, out of mind. The NRPS provide the knowledge and experience to make a TA company run smoothly. The continuity of their presence in a company is invaluable.

"The TA proper are civilians whose hobby is soldiering. Most of them will join at the age of around 19 to 23, and then they make their way up the Territorial Army ladder the same way that they would do if they were regulars. Some do come in from the regular army. They may have left for compassionate reasons, for instance, but still want to do soldiering, so they join the TA. However the TA are civilians first and foremost, and we, the regular army, have to recognise that. If a man says he can't come on Tuesday night because his job won't allow it, then that has to take priority. That's his privilege.

"More is demanded of the TA soldier now than was probably the case ten years ago. The TA officer is expected to devote a lot of time to it. It takes eleven to twelve months to commission a man. If he isn't willing to express his commitment in terms of time devoted to the TA, then he isn't going to get a commission. If a soldier goes for a long period of time without turning up,

then eventually we write and ask him to bring his kit back. You get people who turn up regularly every Tuesday night, every weekend they can, every camp, for years and years. Then at the other end of the scale you get the chap who comes for a few weekends, then finds a girlfriend, and doesn't bother to turn up any more. Some people will come in for a couple of years, leave for a perfectly good reason, then rejoin two years later. For this reason there's great turbulence in the TA. The turnover is something like 30 percent per year.

"5RGJ is a battalion being formed under the Phase 2 enhancement scheme. The timing of it is drawn out. We have to be fully operational, as a battalion, by 1990. We're not starting entirely from scratch. At the moment the 4th Battalion of the Royal Green Jackets is spread across London, Buckinghamshire and Oxfordshire, with Battalion HQ in London. There will be another company in London, and when the split comes it will become the London Green Jacket Battalion. The two county companies of 4RGJ, which are at Aylesbury and Oxford, will hive off and become the Fifth Royal Green Jackets. The size of a TA battalion varies according to where it is and what its role is, whether Nato or home defence roled. We are going to be a 3 company

Below: As part of the One-Army concept, Territorial units have now been issued with exactly the same equipment as their Regular counterparts in this case the Carl Gustav anti-tank weapon system.

battalion, i.e. 3 rifle companies, plus there is also a Headquarters company which includes support platoons. 5RGJ will consist of a rifle company at Aylesbury, another at Milton Keynes, and a third at High Wycombe. Oxford will become Battalion HQ, and HQ Company. We'll be a NATO-roled battalion, with a mortar platoon, a MILAN (anti-tank missile) platoon, and a reconnaissance platoon. Basically, if there's a war, we go across the Channel. Home defence battalions have equipment differences, and don't exercise in Germany. Overseas exercises are one of the attractions for recruits. The Aylesbury company will be going to Germany in 1986. I'll be able to say, 'Join up in September, and three weeks later you'll be at camp in Germany.'"

Selection process

What makes someone join the TA as a recruit? Selection weekends are held three times a year, and include a recruiting film, a run, an assault course exercise, and a written test. A medical examination ensures no-one with obvious handicaps such as a heart condition slips through. Blood tests are taken to establish blood groups for future reference. About a third of those who attend selection weekends decide that the TA is not for them. A further 10 percent are rejected for various reasons. Less than 60 percent go on to become recruits.

Julian Lee is a recruit currently based at the Slade Park TA Centre, Oxford. After about three months attendance, which will include 12 Tuesday night sessions, plus 3 training weekends, he and others from his intake will go to recruit camp. If they pass out successfully from that, demonstrating sufficient aptitude on the SLR rifle, the General Purpose Machine Gun, and also on the drill square, they will qualify to wear their berets and badges for the first time. Julian Lee is 25 years old. "I'm training as a building surveyor, but I've always been interested in the army. I tried to get into the Royal Marines when I was 22, but I failed. I saw an ad in the local press for the TA, saying, 'Come along to a recruiting weekend,' so I went along. I feel that this is an opportunity to see what it's all about. I'll give it a year to see if I really enjoy it. The best bit so far has been doing fieldcraft, and working with the GPMG. You realise that soldiering's an art. It's really interesting to learn it."

Todd Parkhurst is a 19 year old carpenter in the building industry. "I'm in my last four weeks of basic training now. My firm don't like me being in, but they have to put up with it. None of my mates at work would like to commit themselves to it. I get time off from work, but its unpaid. One good thing, it's a complete change of lifestyle. You get away from home, nagging parents etc, and you feel refreshed. I really like the weapons. We had our first go at shooting a couple of weeks ago. It was an experience firing the SLR. I never expected anything so loud or powerful. I was getting a bit fed up. We'd been handling them so long, you want to shoot them. As soon as we got some shooting in I was revived. We've got a weekend exercise coming up

Above: Territorial section commander of the Royal Anglian Regiment communicates with his HQ during a field exercise. Part-time leaders are a vital component of the Territorial system.

on Otmoor, marching, fieldcraft, sentry duty, making hides, sleeping out, all outdoor work. I see myself staying in for the three years, but I haven't experienced all the ups and downs yet. If I'm miserable and hating it . . . this weekend's really going to be the crunch time."

TA soldiers enlist for an initial 3 years, and after that can extend their service by 2, 3 or 4 year engagements. The weekly Training Nights are voluntary, but essential to continuity of training, particularly in the first two years. The recruit also has to attend at least eight training weekends, as well as the compulsory 15 day annual camp. Pay is on a scale slightly lower than that in the regular army, but there is an annual bonus, which has to

be earned by completing the training commitment. It comes in the form of a tax-free bounty, currently £150 in year one, increasing to £400 in the third and subsequent years. In the Home Service Force this bounty consists of £35 in the first year, increasing to £100 in the third year. Some territorials claim that the financial remunerations have no bearing on their motivation, while others find the pay and bounty a very useful addition to their civilian income. The longer your service in the TA, the higher your daily rate, and, as in the regulars, pay goes up with rank. Corporal Robert 'Jock' Amis is 33 years old, works in house-building as a civilian, but has been in the TA for 10 years. "In another two years I get my long service medal. I've jacked some jobs in because they wouldn't give me the time for the TA, and I sometimes take my holidays to coincide with camps and exercises. I make about £24 a day as a corporal with ten years in. My job in the TA is as a weapons instructor for recruits. So far I've been to Germany five times, and Holland once, as well as going on exercises and camps in England and Wales.

"The TA lads work hard these days. Unless you like what you're doing, it's easy to get pissed off. Everything they do is measured against the regulars. For instance, the regulars get a month's basic training on the rifle, and our lads only get 18 hours. What we lack in finesse, we make up in enthusiasm. If you're doing it

Left: Recent experiments within the Territorial Army have included equipping units with Armoured Fighting Vehicles such as this Fox armoured car, armed with a 30 mm Rarden Cannon. Below: Territorial units, along with their Regular counterparts, are progressively trained to fight in a Nuclear environment. Above: Javelin – a revised version of the blowpipe anti-aircraft missile.

just for the money, you're wasting your time. The TA's a challenge, and what you get out is what you put in."

Overseas Units

One innovation in the Phase 2 expansion of the TA has been the setting up of overseas units for the first time. The first unit of the TA ever recruited outside the UK was 408(Berlin) Field Troop Royal Engineers (Volunteer), recruited, as are all the new overseas units, entirely from British passport holders. There were 100 applications for just twenty-eight available places. Other units being formed overseas are an Ambulance Train Staff at Moenchengladbach, a General Transport Squadron at Dusseldorf, an RAOC vehicle platoon and a Defence Animal Support Unit working with guard dogs. HQ BAOR has had to bring out special dual language pamphlets explaining the workings of the 'British Reserve Army' for the benefit of German employers, who, like British employers at home in the UK, are encouraged to give time to employees serving in the TA.

The importance of the TA to British defence is out of all proportion to both its image until recent years, and its cost. A good 50 percent of the British army's mobilised strength consists of a combination of the individual reservists – ex-regulars with statutory reserve time still being served, – and the territorials. The Individual reservists number some 100,000 to the TA's 76,500, but are not in the same state of 48 hour preparedness that applies to the modern TA soldier. Nor are they as regularly trained and kept up to date. 75% of the TA has a NATO role, providing, as we have seen, a very large percentage of the medical, logistic and infantry support provided by BAOR. The new status of the TA within army thinking is reflected in a new level of equipment. The time gap between the army receiving new equipment, and the TA receiving it, is narrowing rapidly. The first airborn TA unit is being formed, a helicopter squadron using Scout Helicopters, based at Middle Wallop, and manned by ex-regulars with helicopter experience. Two of the Yeomanry regiments now have Scimitar tracked vehicles, the first time TA units have ever had Armoured Personnel Carriers (APCs). The TA is now scheduled to be issued with the new LAW-80 infantry anti-tank weapon. The MILAN anti-tank weapon was issued to TA battalions with a BAOR role before it was issued to regulars with a home defence role. It featured extensively in the Lionheart exercise in Germany in 1984. The high profile of TA participants in Lionheart, and later, in the UK based Brave Defender exercise, may have had a significant effect on improved recruiting figures for the TA. Also on the equipment side, a new TA Javelin Air Defence Regiment is being formed, bringing to three the number of TA regiments equipped with Javelin, in place of the Blowpipe systems they had previously.

The expansion of the TA's size and role has a knock-on effect on its members. Greater importance means more exercises, better equipment, and, inevitably, a greater level of interest and enthusiasm. The turnover rate, at 30 percent per year is still high, but those that stay are keen and involved. After six years it is reckoned a TA soldier is hooked for the duration. The problem then could be persauding them to leave when they reach the age limit.

The Royal Naval Reserve

The Royal Navy is the Senior Service, and the Royal Naval Reserve is the oldest of the auxiliary services, dating its official origins back to 1859, when an Act of Parliament established a Reserve Force of merchant seamen and officers. Of all the auxiliary services, the RNR is to be increased by the greatest proportion in the expansion set in motion by the Ministry of Defence. By 1991 the RNR's strength is to be increased by almost 40 percent, from its current level of over 5,600, to around 7,800. This will represent some 12 percent of the Royal Navy's mobilised strength. However in certain specific tasks the RNR's input will be far larger. Mine Counter Measures (MCM) is the RNR's major task, and in time of war it would man around 60 percent of the Navy's MCM forces.

The RNR is organised into eleven Divisions around the coast of the UK. These are Tay (at Dundee), Forth (Edinburgh), Tyne (Gateshead), London, Sussex (Hove), Solent (Southampton), Severn (Bristol), South Wales (Sully), Mersey (Liverpool), Ulster (Belfast), and Clyde (Glasgow). Most of the country's major ports are covered in this way, with an operational RNR unit in each. All of these divisions are Sea Training Centres for the RNR, with a catchment area of about 40 miles around each one, though some volunteers travel farther than this. In addition to the Divisions are seven Headquarters Units, which are control and planning centres for naval and NATO sea exercises, based at Naval Shore Headquarters. RNR personnel support the Royal Navy staff at the shore HQs, and could work alongside, and if necessary, replace them in time of war. Reservists at these HQ units have to live close by. There are also twelve inland training centres. They are communications training centres, though other types of training can be given at them.

The sea exerts a particular sort of influence upon those who live or work near it and on it. Generally, those who join the navy or its reserves have an element of this attraction in their make-up, as well as all the other motivations that lead men and women to join other services, like patriotism, and the need to feel challenged, or the need for companionship, or a taste for things military. Many reservists over the years have been merchant seamen, or yachtsmen, or have come from the fishing industry. Others were born near the sea, or on estuaries. Many more have come from inland, but have developed an involvement with the sea that never seems to recede. Once hooked, that's it. London Division of the RNR is based aboard a pair of 'Flower' class sloops built in 1917 to look like merchant ships and fool the German navy. The Division establishment is known as HMS *President*, and embraces both of these venerable vessels, now moored slightly upstream from Blackfriars Bridge on the Thames. The ships themselves are named HMS *President* (once HMS *Saxifrage*), and HMS *Chrysanthemum*, and they are a well-known part of the London landscape. At some time in 1987 London Division is due to move to new, shore-based premises in the refurbished St Catherine's Dock.

HMS President

Simon Vernon was born in the Midlands but is in love with the sea. In civilian life he is a chartered surveyor, but he has been in the RNR for four years, and on training nights climbs the steps over the wall on the Thames Embankment and walks the gangplank to board HMS *President*. He is an RO-1, a radio operator. He first joined up in Bristol, at HMS *Flying Fox*, the training centre for Severn Division. All RNR volunteers are trained as specialists of one sort or another. Simon Vernon started out in the Operations – Seaman Branch, but after a year was allowed to switch to Operations – Communications. His full title is Radio Operator 1 (Tactical), which means that he specialises in the communications necessary for the tactical operations and manoeuvring of ships at sea. This is 'bridge-work', and embraces voice, automatic telegraphy and visual communications (such as lights and flags). Like other new recruits, Simon started off at *Flying Fox* with a period of basic training in naval matters, from marching and saluting to ship identification and ropework. Dinghy-sailing experience stood him in good stead. Reservists turn up for training once or twice a week, and also attend some weekends. Once a year they have to carry out a fourteen-day unbroken training period, which enables them to attend specialist courses or go out on extended sea-training exercises. (These are men only, as the Women's RNR is shore-based). Simon Vernon's first annual fortnight was spent in the Mediterranean, carrying out mine-sweeping exercises aboard HMS *Venturer*, a fishing vessel converted to minesweeper.

Working in a squadron of six sweepers, HMS *Venturer* moved from Sicily, to Gibraltar, and on to Lisbon. The mines they swept were layed by HMS *Abdiel*, which was manned by a regular RN crew. Simon moved to London as his civilian job dictated, transferring from HMS *Flying Fox* to HMS *President*, and beginning his communications training. After four years in the RNR he is keener than ever, and intends to work his way up the ladder, maybe doing further training in navigation.

Approximately 8 would-be recruits walk aboard HMS *President* every week to see what it is all about, having seen the RNR notice-board outside as they walked along the Embankment. On average 5 are men, and 3 are women. In addition to this 'passing trade', the recruiting office aboard *President* receives an annual 500 to 600 paper applications, many from people responding to local press advertisements.

Above: RNR recruits prepare to fire a line from one vessel to another at sea. The Eighties have seen an increase in the activities of the Naval Reserve forces.

Full time to part time

The other main source of recruits are ex-naval servicemen. With this amount of applications, the recruiting office is kept so busy that the staff have to work Saturdays every so often just to keep the backlog of paperwork clear. Yet all these applications boil down eventually to 3 new entry classes a year, with maybe 30 recruits in each class. After 3 or 4 months these recruits will attend HMS *Raleigh* at Devonport for an instruction fortnight that includes classes in history and ceremony, and instruction in seamanship, fire-fighting, and damage control. There are drill periods every day, and the RNR recruits are treated the same as RN trainees, with strict discipline. Survival exercises in wild countryside, and assault courses are tackled during the fortnight.

HMS *President* is an exceptionally busy centre, 'at work' every day, and with a permanent staff of about thirty. These include some RN officers, and a comple-

ment of MOD ship-keepers. Any reservist living close by could find something to do practically every day. Lieutenant Paul Kennerley, the President's PR Officer, points out that the centre is in fact the only Naval presence in London. For this reason it takes part in a large number of ceremonial events, such as Remembrance Day, and the Lord Mayor's Show. Lt. Kennerley has been in the RNR for some 15 years.

"I joined in 1970/71, going through the normal recruiting procedure, going to the lower decks as an ordinary seaman. This was in Newcastle, Tyne Division. I'd been in for about 3 months before I was sent off to sea for a two-week training period, in a *'Ton'* class minesweeper. There was a crew of about 40 to 45, and I was put in the stokers' mess, which was something of a shock to my system. There was no running water down below. You ate down there and slept down there. It was extremely basic. In those days we took our minesweeping fortnights from Portsmouth, and normally were in amongst a squadron of *'Ton'* class minesweepers. You'd do eight or nine days sweeping, and then peel off and go off on a 'jolly', somewhere on the way home – probably a foreign visit. We stopped at Emden in Germany, and had a terrific welcome. After that I came to London Division where I've been ever since. After about 3 years I became an Able Seaman, and then I was selected for promotion to become an officer." Paul Kennerley discovered at the medical for probationary acting sub-lieutenant that he had defective eyesight, which debarred him from qualifying as an executive officer. Undaunted, he carried on, and eventually went on a Divisional Officer's course at Dartmouth for two weeks.

"I couldn't believe what a superb place that was. There was total involvement in the navy. Everyone was at the peak of fitness, keeness, involvement. I was sailing every day, swimming every day, and we had riding lessons with the Marines at Lympstone. I became completely immersed in the whole thing there. We also went on the Tarzan assault course at Lympstone, which was a pretty harrowing experience, but very good for us. We don't do enough of that sort of thing. After two more years I became an acting sub-lieutenant. I went into the Naval Control of Shipping (NSC) side of things. That involves the control and support of merchant shipping, which is a very specialist RNR activity. The RN has virtually nothing to do with that. Amongst NATO countries the Brits are the only people qualified to undertake this sort of duty. I became a sub-lieutenant. My first fortnight's training as an NCS officer took me to NATO, Portugal, to what was then Commander Iberian Atlantic, who was an American rear-admiral. I found myself in the whole new world of NATO. Some of the most interesting parts of it were at the daily admiral's briefing, to hear the real live intelligence which they'd found. If we had a convoy at sea, which we sometimes did on those exercises, you would hear who was actually tracking them, Warsaw Pact ships, submarines, aeroplanes etc."

As an NCS officer Lt. Kennerley was involved in the routing of merchant ships through the NATO exercise sea area, making sure they were safe, and not steaming through firing and mining areas. He has been back to Lisbon about four times since then. He is now a boarding officer, and on an exercise would be required to board ships at sea or in harbour, to brief or debrief the ships' masters. His NCS duties have taken him to Portugal, to Scotland, to the Port of London area, and to Felixstowe.

Back at HMS *President* Lt. Kennerley has been, among other duties, sports and 'pulling' officer – pulling being the technical term for rowing the heavy Montague whalers in which the unit takes part once a year in the Fishmongers' Cup. The race runs from Lambeth Bridge to HMS *President* or vice versa, depending on the tide. The RNR pulls against the Royal Marine Reserve, the River Police, and the Fire Brigade. He is now Public Relations Officer. He attends at *President* two evenings a week, works many weekends, and still goes to sea as

a 2nd Officer of the Watch, often going out to Alderney, Jersey, Cherbourg, or on day runs out of Portsmouth, helping navigate and plot positions, and taking over the bridge when necessary. This is the work he really enjoys, and says that this is what he joined for.

Minesweeping

In 1986 four mine-sweeping fortnights were arranged for the men of HMS *President*, which meant four separate crews were formed to work in HMS *Humber*, London Division's new *River* class mine-sweeper. The fortnights were based on Gibraltar. One crew took the *Humber* down to the Mediterranean, swept for their alloted period and were then handed over to the second crew and so on. The replacement crews flew out, and the replaced crews flew back. HMS *Humber* was commissioned in June 1985, and is one of the twelve *River* class Minesweepers Fleet (MSFs) being introduced for sole use by the RNR. The RNR's minesweepers form the 10th Minesweeping Squadron, which works alongside the Royal Navy in peace and war, crewed entirely by reserves. Specialising in deep-water sweeping, the RNR ships work in teams, using underwater wires to cut the cables of buoyancy mines, and towing cables that can emit electrical impulses to explode magnetic mines. Towed noisemakers are used to detonate acoustic mines. Some ships, including the MSFs, can be equipped as mine hunters, using electronic means such as sonar to locate sea-bed and other mines ahead of the ship. The mine hunters use mine-disposal weapons to explode mines discovered in this way, and carry a team of clearance divers. Most mine-hunting is done by the Royal Navy, though RN ships engaged in hunting carry RNR crew members often.

The new MSFs were developed specifically for their role as a result of experience gained in two trawler conversions, the *Venturer* and the *St David*. They are replacing the old *'Ton'* class ('*Coniston*' class) Mine Counter Measures Vessels (MCMVs) which gave many young officers their first commands, and were ideal training ships for all crews. The *River* class MSFs are built by Richards of Lowestoft in close cooperation with the Naval Staff. 156 feet (47.6 metres) in length, with a beam of 34 feet (10.5 metres), and a loaded draft of 11 feet (3.4 metres), the MSFs displace 780 tonnes, and are powered by two Ruston 6RKCM engines developing 1520 Bhp each. They carry a war complement of about 30, usually consisting of 7 officers, 7 Senior Ratings, and 16 Junior Ratings.

In 1985 three MSFs, HMS *Carron* from Severn Division, HMS *Waveney* from South Wales Division, and HMS *Dovey* from Clyde Division, crossed the Atlantic together unescorted, each crewed by 34 reservists, to take part in the 75th anniversary of Canada's Naval Service, at Halifax, Nova Scotia. After the celebrations the MSFs took part in sweeping exercises. During the course of Maplehaul 85, as the expedition was known, two changeovers of crews took place, so that in all over

Above: HMS *Glasserton, Ton* Class Minesweeper drawn up alongside HMS *Chrysanthemum* on the Thames embankment.

300 RNR members were able to participate. The RNR ships were greatly admired by the representatives of the eleven other countries with ships attending the Canadian celebrations, and Prince Andrew represented the Queen at the review.

As well as the MSFs, the RNR also employs 'Tracker' class fast patrol boats for navigational and general seamanship training. In time of war these would serve for harbour defence, and could also act as navigational leaders for MCM operations, guiding convoys and ships through channels swept in minefields. They have a range of 650 nautical miles at a cruising speed of 20 knots, and accommodate a crew of eleven. A new fast patrol boat, the P2000 is now also in use by the RNR, similar in size and power to the Trackers. One role foreseen for them is as manoeuvrable, shallow water patrollers able to seek out and counter possible coastal attacks by small groups of Soviet Speznaz troops in time of war.

The Royal Naval Auxiliary Service

Wendy Gibson is a quiet young woman who works in market research during the week. On Wednesday evenings she puts on the uniform of the Royal Naval Auxiliary Service (RNXS) and travels to The Royal Naval College beside the River Thames at Greenwich. There, up in the attic of Christopher Wren's magnificent building, she instructs RNXS volunteers in the complexities of such tasks as naval chartwork, and the writing of signals. Wendy bears the rank of Leading Naval Auxiliaryman (LNX). In time of war she would go to the local Port Headquarters (PHQ) and slot immediately and expertly into her support role with the Naval Officer in Charge, helping coordinate the mind-boggling intricacies of coastal traffic, and liaising with other home defence organisations, including harbour authorities, HMS Coastguard, and the police. LNX Gibson has trained for this job on numerous weekend exercises. Like other

Auxiliarymen she has developed a formidable local knowledge which is one of the key strengths of this unusual service.

"I originally wanted to join the Navy, but it didn't work out at the time I left school. I joined the RNXS in 1980 as a good compromise. There's no naval history in my family at all as far as I know, but it has always interested me. I love anything to do with the sea. I joined the RNXS in October 1980. A friend of mine had joined in response to an advertisement, and she introduced me. You do an introductory period, during which the various subjects are explained, and you can show if you've got any aptitudes. There's a small exam at the end. You learn about the work of the RNXS, which includes a Communications Branch, and Operations Branch, and Afloat Duties."

Captain John Griffiths RN inhabits an office deep in the bowels of a windswept Naval fort overlooking Portsmouth, but is seldom to be found there. As Captain, Royal Naval Auxiliary Service, a post to which he was appointed in November 1984, a great part of his year is spent travelling, literally, the length and breadth of the country visiting in turn the 72 units of the RNXS. It is a job, like the painting of the Forth Bridge, which has no ending, but one to which he is obviously devoted. The units are grouped in twos, threes and fours to support their local Port Headquarters, from Lerwick in the Shetlands to Guernsey in the Channel Islands, and from the east coast of England to Belfast in Ulster. The smallest unit, in Stornoway in the Hebrides has just seven volunteers, while Merseyside, the largest, has close to a hundred.

"Fundamentally, we are a civilian, uniformed, unarmed, unpaid force of volunteers, whose role is to support the Royal Navy in the ports and anchorages around the United Kingdom. There are about 2,800 volunteers at the moment, located at the 72 training centres. Some are co-located with PHQs, and some are co-located with the RNR, in sea-training and communications-training centres. About one in four of the volunteers are female. There is an Afloat Branch as well as the Ashore

tasks. Ashore they support the Naval Officer in Charge, basically in operations room and communications duties, maintaining plots and state-boards, manning teleprinters, manning voice-radio circuits, both for the Naval Control of Merchant Shipping (NCS), and in support of the Defence of Ports and Anchorages (DEFPA). Afloat we've got a flotilla at the moment of ten of the old 'Loyal' class fleet tenders, and we used to have two of the former inshore minesweepers, which are being phased out, and replaced by the P2000 Watercraft, similar to the 'Archer' class of the RNR, except that our four have black hulls instead of grey ones. We have a problem in the expansion of the Afloat side, announced in last year's Defence White Paper (SDE 85), as a two thirds increase in the Afloat side to cope with the fact that we have been asked to take on one third of the DEFPA task. To do that we have to expand our present training capacity. If we increase Afloat by two thirds, we need a pro rata increase in training capacity available. So we're asking a follow-on class of vessels. We have an agreed requirement, and it's now a question of the Naval Staff finding funds within the Naval Programme to meet it. If we don't get it, we can't do it. We don't have a budget. We're the original parasites. We live off everyone else's budgets. The Operational side is rather different. When you get to a state of emergency, when the Government can take emergency powers, then we can requisition craft from trade. We can provide the hulls if we've got the people to put in them who are trained."

Afloat Branch

Mike Fisher is 47 years old, works as a civil engineer, and has been in the RNXS for six years. He is now an 'A' level Seaman in the Afloat Branch, based at the Greenwich unit.

"There's no family connection with the Navy. I've always been interested in merchant ships, and my father worked for the Port of London Authority. As a child I lived at Tilbury, within 50 yards of the river bank, and was interested in the ships going past, and all the different lines. I came across the RNXS at Chatham. I thought I might be of some use, so I came and talked to the Head of the unit here, explained what my interests were, and that I'd like to get involved. He asked me if I had a preference for which side I served on, and I said I'd like to go afloat, and he said there were vacancies on the Afloat side so long as I passed the medical. Since then I've certainly been pleased with my choice, particularly on exercises on the Thames. I find it particularly interesting, having lived alongside the river previously. When circumstances allow I think I'd like to try for mate. You have to do a lot of work on your own to go for that. It's a watch-keeping certificate issued by the Department of Trade. When you first go afloat you have to learn deckwork, 'evolutions' as they're called, involving raising and lowering the anchor, a spell at the wheel, ship's husbandry – looking after the ship, and doing

cleaning and painting, that sort of thing. Later on you have to learn assistant watch-keeping, radar, chart-work, and then passage planning, taking more and more responsibility as you go towards mate. Eventually of course, as a mate, in an emergency you can take over a vessel." Mike Fisher has trained mainly in inshore minesweepers and fleet tenders, and is looking forward enthusiastically to working aboard the new P2000.

There is something very reassuring about the men and women who volunteer for the RNXS. Most are not 'steely-eyed' in the sense that they want to carry arms and hanker after the sharp end of conflict. They have chosen to join an organisation where the average age of a unit can be in the mid-forties, where there is no statutory commitment to minimum service requirements, and where money plays little or no part in things - pay-rates and annual bonuses are not part of the RNXS scheme of things, though basic expenses are paid to ensure volunteers are not out of pocket in attending training nights and weekends. Despite this they are disciplined and highly skilled. The war-time roles for which they train are completely essential to the overall defence programme. They radiate a great affection for the sea and ships. Above all what comes across when talking to them is their deep desire to protect something very dear to them.

1987 is the year when the RNXS celebrates its Silver Jubilee.

The Royal Auxiliary Airforce

In 1984 the Royal Auxiliary Airforce (RAuxAF) celebrated the 60th anniversary of its formation. It was able to underline this Diamond Jubilee by taking part in the LIONHEART Exercise, represented by its Auxiliary Air Movements Squadron and Auxiliary Aeromedical Evacuation Squadron, both of which were formed in 1983, and part of a general expansion of the RAuxAF which seems certain to continue in the foreseeable future. As in the TA and the RNR, volunteers are paid at a rate close to that of the regular RAF on a pro-rata basis, and have to fulfil a taxing requirement of weekend training exercises and annual camps to prepare themselves for the defence roles they are expected to fulfil.

The RAuxAf has an impressive series of 'firsts' to its credit. As the Auxiliary AF, with 20 squadrons to its name at the time of the outbreak of war in 1939, it soon became the first arm of the services to bring down a German aircraft over Britain, on October 16 of the same year. The AuxAF was also the first British organisation to use jet fighters, and the pilots of 616 (South Yorkshire) Squadron flew the new Meteors against the V1 flying bombs, which they 'tipped' over, wing-tip to wing-tip to make them crash before they reached their population targets. It was the AuxAF which sank the first U-boat with the help of air-to-surface radar. Perhaps the most visible role of the AuxAF in World War II was its deployment of 1500 barrage balloons. At the end of the war King George VI granted the AuxAF

Above: A patrol of 2624 Squadron Royal Auxiliary Air Force Regiment whose task is to defend air installations in Britain against enemy or subversive attack.

Above: A woman member of the R Aux AF Regt on signalling duties in a mobile command post. Regulars and Auxiliaries are increasingly interchangeable.

the prefix 'Royal', in recognition of its wartime service.

After the war the barrage balloon squadrons were disbanded, and the auxiliary flying squadrons followed suit in 1957, as the MOD was reluctant to issue supersonic aircraft to non-regulars. RAuxAF volunteers in the three remaining units continued to train up to full operational standards, supporting regulars at the three joint Naval/Air Maritime HQs at Northwood, Edinburgh and Plymouth, especially in intelligence and communications operations.

Since 1979 the RAuxAF has benefitted from the new MOD thinking on volunteer services, with the formation in that year of three RAuxAF Regiment Field Squadrons specifically for the defence of front-line RAF airfields and ground installations in Britain. The trial run was a great success, and three more RAuxAF Regiment Field Squadrons followed. Personnel train to the very high standards of the regular RAF Regiment, and are equipped with up to date infantry weapons.

The only RAuxAF squadron directly connected to air traffic is No 4624 (County of Oxford) RAuxAF Movements Squadron at Brize Norton, which it is planned to expand to eight flights. Some members have served on detachment on Ascension Island, helping out with the constant traffic and load movements at this staging post

for the Falkland Islands. On September 9 1983 an entirely new departure for the RAuxAF was instituted with the formation of No4626 (County of Wiltshire) Aeromedical Evacuation Squadron, designed to provide medical skills for use during air evacuations.

Flying role wanted

What most people in the RAuxAF would like to see is the reintroduction of a flying role for their volunteers. As it is, members put in an exceptionally high training commitment, completing on average 150 hours a year of non-continuous training, as well as the fifteen day continuous requirement in the form of exercises and camps. There is no doubt that recruitment for flying squadrons would be faced with the problem of over application. Occasionally rumours are heard of a possible auxiliary Wessex support helicopter squadron, which might be forthcoming, according to the 1985 Defence White Paper, "as soon as the resources are available". So far there is no sign of these resources, and the most recent new expansion has been the formation of a new squadron at RAF Waddington to be trained in the operation of the Skyguard anti-aircraft system captured in mint condition from the Argentine forces during the Falklands war.

Chapter 6

AIR WAR: THE PLANE-MAKERS

With today's combat aircraft costing many millions of pounds a piece, it is becoming ever harder for individual manufacturers, or even nations, to equip the air forces in sufficient quantities at an acceptable cost. Thus, countries and companies combine to pool requirements and resources to produce the ultimate hybrid.

Tornado aircraft in the final assembly hall at BAe Warton.

On 9 January 1986, the British Secretary of State for Defence, Michael Heseltine, resigned from the Thatcher government as a result of his distaste for the way in which the Cabinet was handling the 'Westland Affair'. By the date of Heseltine's resignation, Westland Helicopters PLC, Britain's major helicopter manufacturer, was on the point of total collapse if a financial rescue package could not be quickly organised. Two options were available, a company-backed solution based around a link up with the American firm Sikorsky and the Italian Fiat group and an option proposed by a European consortium of the German MBB, the French Aerospatiale, the Italian Agusta and the British GEC and British Aerospace concerns. Heseltine's complaints were twofold, namely his fervent belief in the European option which was being all but ignored by the Westland board and his dismay at the Government's policy of 'even-handedness' towards the two packages being, as he saw it, publicly promoted on the one hand whilst in private favouring the Sikorsky deal.

The 'Westland Affair' has already cost another minister his job, threatened the Prime Minister herself and shows signs of rumbling on for some considerable time. Whilst this sad saga might at first sight appear to have little connection with the subject matter of this chapter, in fact it is an admirable illustration of the dilemma facing the free world's aviation industries; the brutally simple fact that no one company or nation (with the possible exception of the United States) can easily fund a modern combat aircraft alone.

Cost explosion

As sweeping as such a statement might appear, it is none the less true. Some idea of the enormity of the problem can be gained from the US defence budget for Fiscal Year 1986 (October 1985 to October 1986), during which, Congress has approved an overall expenditure of $281.2 billion on arms. Contained within this staggeringly large sum is $23.546 billion for aircraft and $8.43 billion for missile procurement by the USAF, $6.578 billion for combat aircraft procurement and $1.865 billion for aircraft modification programmes within the USN and $3.567 billion for aircraft procurement by the US Army. Such figures are almost beyond common comprehension and it is only when one considers that the total figure quoted is probably larger than the gross national product of a typical third world country and that the total of $43.986 billion the US intends to spend on aerospace during the period is almost twice as much as the UK spent in total on defence during 1984/85 that any sort of perspective concerning them can be gained.

The cost explosion within the military aerospace field is in fact a relatively recent phenomenon which, in the broadest of terms, can be traced back to the emergence of 'weapons systems' rather than straightforward fighters and bombers during the late Fifties and early Six-

ties. Because of factors such as monetary inflation, technological advance and the blurring of traditional operational categories, it is extremely difficult to present accurate comparative data to illustrate this point. With this in mind however, it is still perhaps instructive to consider three major fighter aircraft used by the RAF between 1939 and the present day.

From Spitfire to Tornado

At the beginning of World War II, the service's premier daylight interceptor was the Supermarine Spitfire Mk I. For its day, the Spitfire was at the forefront of fighter technology being a monoplane equipped with a retractable undercarriage and using metal construction throughout. Power was provided by a single Rolls Royce Merlin II 12-cylinder piston engine driving a three-bladed propellor. The pilot was housed in an enclosed but unpressurised cockpit equipped with flying controls, engine and navigational instruments, an optical gunsight and an air-to-air/air-to-ground radio. The Spitfire's armament comprised eight rifle calibre machine guns and the type could reach a maximum speed of 346mph (557km/hr) at 15,000ft (4,575m).

Seventeen years later in 1956, the RAF began to re-

Above: 241 Squadron Spitfire Mark IXs patrol Mount Vesuvius in Italy in 1943.

ceive examples of the jet powered Hawker Hunter F Mk 6 interceptor. Whilst the Hunter represented a quantum leap in terms of performance over the Spitfire, in reality, it was little more than a jet propelled equivalent being designed for the same daylight interception role. Using the same criteria as for the described Spitfire Mk I, the Hunter F Mk 6 was powered by a single 10,150 lb st (4,605kgp) thrust Rolls Royce Avon 207 turbojet, giving it a maximum speed of close to Mach 1 at 36,000ft (10,973m). The pilot was now housed in a pressurised enclosed cockpit and seated on an ejection seat. Armament remained of the gun type (in this case two 30mm Aden cannon) and the type was equipped with state-of-the art communications and a simple ranging radar set.

Jumping forward a further 28 years, the RAF began to take delivery of its latest interceptor, the Panavia Tornado F Mk 2. Comparison with the earlier aeroplanes is almost impossible as this new two seater exceeds and adds to their capabilities in a way which places it light years away from even its immediate predecessors let alone the described types. The new aeroplane is designed for long range interception in all weather conditions and employs the latest technological advances, such as a 'swing' wing, to achieve the re-

Above: Hawker Hunter F6 of 234 Sqn, 229 Operational Conversion Unit at RAF Chivenor in April 1974. Below: A Panavia Tornado F2 rolls out of its hangar into the morning sunlight at RAF Coningsby. When 'clean', i.e. unencumbered with external weapons and stores, the aircraft can achieve speeds in excess of Mach 2.

quired performance. Powered by two Turbo-Union RB199-34R Mk 103 afterburning turbojets, the Tornado can achieve a maximum speed of Mach 2.16 in level flight when 'clean', that is not encumbered with external stores. To aid the crew in the interception task, the aeroplane is equipped with a battery of electronic aids ranging from the powerful GEC Avionics AI-24 Foxhunter radar which can detect targets out to a range of 115mls (185km), through an 'IFF' system which can electronically identify 'friends' and 'foes' to a wide range of voice/data communication and navigation systems.

Major systems advance

Crew aids do not stop with the described systems as they are provided with a range of flight control systems which both ease the pilot's work load and cope with such things as optimising the angle of the wings for the particular flight regime required. The movement forward in systems and performance has been equally matched by the aircraft's armament which comprises four Sky Flash semi-active radar homing air-to-air missiles, a 27mm IWKA-Mauser cannon and up to two infra red homing AIM-9L Sidewinder air-to-air missiles.

It is the author's opinion that the three cited examples illustrate both the enormous technological advances whch have taken place since World War II and the central problem of funding and developing systems like the Tornado very well as, whilst there are no accurate price comparisons available for the purchase of a single

Spitfire and a single Tornado, it is probably fair to say that one of the latter's Sky Flash missiles will cost as much as a 1939 Spitfire Mk I! Even then, sheer expense is not the only problem confronting today's military aircraft designers. As the brief outline of the Tornado given earlier hopefully shows, it is a system incorporating many disciplines (electronics, aerodynamics, engine technology, displays and the like) and a given company or indeed country frequently does not have access to the necessary expertise.

The answer to this general dilemma has been known for some time but has not been easy to achieve. Up until the Sixties, the European nations still found it possible to develop nationally or buy in the aircraft deemed necessary for their defence but the writing was already on the wall. Co-operation within NATO was the obvious answer with all the relevant air forces pooling their resources to purchase a common type for a particular role and thereby generate a level of production which would effectively reduce costs. The first attempt at such a programme was in fact made during the late Fifties when NATO held a competition for an attack aircraft to be used by its European members. The winner of this competition was the Italian G.91 lightweight strike fighter but in the event, the 'Gina', as the aircraft be-

A Tornado air defence variant F2 fighter from the first
Operational Conversion Unit for the type at RAF
Conningsby, in Lincolnshire.

came known to its German operators, only entered service with the Italian air force and the newly re-
established Luftwaffe in the German Federal Republic.

Sale of the Century

More successful was what has become known as the
'sale of the century' in which the American aerospace
manufacturer Lockheed sold a quantity of F-104G Starfighter aircraft to the Germans and established a multi-
national European consortium to build the type. This
consortium went on to produce 977 examples of the aircraft which served with the air forces of Germany, the
Netherlands, Italy (who went a stage further and opti-
mised the design for their specific needs under the designation F-104S), Belgium, Denmark, Norway, Turkey and Greece. Not all of these nations were actively
involved in the production programme but all benefitted
from it. Whilst the Starfighter was an American design
and was built under licence in Europe, the 'off-set' of
home production meant that the various countries involved could obtain a high performance combat aircraft
which as single entities they most probably would not
have been able to afford.

This concept of 'bulk buying' combined with 'off-set'
arrangements has been continued in the European F-16

Above: Italian Air Force G91 tactical strike and
reconnaissance aircraft, manufactured by Aeritalia and in
service with Italian and German forces.

Fighting Falcon programme. Under an agreement
reached in 1975, a total of 348 F-16 aircraft would be
built in Europe for the Dutch, Belgian, Danish and
Norwegian air forces. Two production lines were established with the Belgian company SABCA building the
aircraft for their own and the Danish air forces and Fok-
ker producing those for the Dutch and Norwegian services. Further advantage was gained by the Europeans

Above: US-built F16 Fighting Falcon aircraft of the Royal Netherlands Air Force, which are replacing the earlier F104 Starfighters in the inventories of a number of European air forces (below). The Falcon is proving to be the highest selling light fighter aircraft of the Eighties, with markets not only in the industrialised West, but the Third World as well.

in that the production agreement stipulated that European companies would not only work on their own aircraft but would also supply components for USAF F-16s and those sold to Third World air forces.

Like the Starfighter programme before it, this agreement provided four European air forces with a high performance combat aircraft at a relatively reasonable cost and without causing damage to their national aerospace industries. The term 'relatively' is emphasised with regard to the cost effectiveness of the programme as a whole because of the $471,000 'research and development' levy which General Dynamics charged on each of the European F-16s. At the time of the agreement, this meant that each European example cost $6.09 million as against the approximately $4.7 million being charged for USAF examples. Part of this discrepancy can be explained by the agreed levy and part by the costs of setting-up the European production line. Nonetheless, such an arrangement shows clearly that such co-production deals have to be considered very carefully and that the Americans do not do their allies any favours when it comes to the supply of arms unless it is very much in their own interests, a factor which seems not to be readily understood in the UK.

The 'one way' nature of the supposed 'two way' street' in arms sales between Europe and America together with the rapidly developing adverse relationship between escalating systems costs and diminishing defence budgets finally forced the Europeans to consider multi-national production programmes based around original designs. The term 'forced' is sadly all too accurate because the two major aircraft manufacturing countries within the region, Britain and France, have proved not to make the happiest of bed fellows.

Anglo-French enmity

French chauvinism and British isolationism have and continue to make co-operation of any kind between the two countries, despite their common membership of the EEC, difficult. In the Aerospace field, these difficulties have been exacerbated by the success of the French industry on the world's combat aircraft markets and the strength of the economic axis within the EEC between France and Germany. Indeed, this latter factor led to the first modern European success story in multi-national aircraft production, the Transall C-160 military transport.

The Transall (Transporter Allianz) group was formed in January 1959 and comprised the German MBB and VFW concerns together with the French Aerospatiale company. The aim of the consortium was to design, develop and produce a twin turboprop transport for use by the French and German air forces and under the designation C-160, a prototype of such an aircraft made its maiden flight in France on 25 February 1963. This aircraft was followed by two German-built prototypes

Below: C160 Transaal transport aircraft jointly manufactured by MBB of West Germany and Aerospatiale.

during 1963 and early 1964 and the first production examples were delivered to the French (C-160F) and German (C-160D) air forces during 1967 and 1968 respectively.

Capable of carrying up to 93 troops, 81 paratroops or 62 stretchers, a total of 160 C-160D and F aircraft have been delivered to the two services with the Luftwaffe's examples being flown by two transport groups and the Armee de l'Air's by three squadrons. On the export market, 9 Transall aircraft (under the designation C-160Z) have been supplied to South Africa and in 1971, the Luftwaffe transferred 20 such aircraft to the Turkish air force under the designation C-160T.

Production of C-160 ended in 1972 but was re-started four years later with the signing of a new agreement between MBB and Aerospatiale on 29 October 1976. This re-opening of the production line was in response to additional orders for the French air force. The so-called 'second series' C-160s differ from their predecessors in having up-dated avionics and additional fuel tankage to extend the type's range. The first 'second series' aircraft was delivered to the French air force in December 1981 and by 1982, an additional four examples had been added to the original requirement for 25 aircraft. These additional machines are particularly interesting as they are to be equipped with American VLF (Very Low Frequency) transmission gear to support France's nuclear missile submarine force. These 'Astarte' aircraft are not

the only 'special duties' C-160s under development and conversion kits/modification programmes are being offered for a maritime surveillance model (the C-160S), an electronic surveillance version (C-160SE) and an airborne early warning platform (C-160AAA) which uses the GEC Avionics 'Skyguardian' avionics/radar suite.

Although essentially a Franco-German project, the Transall programme has and continues to involve Britain indirectly in that the C-160 is powered by Rolls-Royce Tyne turboprop engines, produced jointly by the British company together with SNECMA, MTU and FN-Herstal. Direct Franco-British co-operation came about in the Sixties with three major programmes, namely the Hawker Siddeley Dynamics/Matra Martel air-launched missile begun in 1964, the Sepecat Jaguar tactical support/trainer aircraft of 1965 and the three helicopter co-production deal of 1967 between Westland and Aerospatiale.

Enter the Jaguar

Without doubt, the most successful of these programmes was the Jaguar. Based on a design produced by the French company Breguet, the Jaguar appeared as a multi-role type configured for tactical battlefield support

Below: A Sepecat Jaguar GR1 of 20 Squadron RAF based at Bruggen in West Germany. Based on a French design, later variants of the Jaguar have, like the US F-16, found a wide market in the developing countries.

and advanced/operational crew training. By the end of 1981, a total of 402 aircraft had been delivered to the two air forces with 202 going to the RAF and 200 to the Armee de l'Air. The success of the design has led to the Jaguar International model configured specifically for the export market. Fitted with up-rated engines, the 'International' offers a wide range of customer options which include provision for Matra Magic or other air-to-air missiles, multi-purpose radars such as the Thomson-CSF Agave, up to four anti-shipping missiles and night/bad weather sensor systems such as low light TV.

The first export Jaguar Internationals went to Ecuador who received 12 examples between January and November 1977, followed by a further dozen which went to Oman between March 1977 and July 1978. By far the biggest order was placed in the following year, when, during 1979, India contracted for the type together with a licence to produce it. The first 40 examples were purchased directly from Britain and were delivered between July 1979 and the end of 1982. Licence production was also stated on a second batch of 45 aircraft by Hindustan Aeronautics at Bangalore using European-built components with the first such aeroplane making its initial flight on 31 March 1982. The Jaguar entered service with the Indian air force during the summer of 1980 and the contract will be completed with the delivery of a third batch of aircraft (31) produced completely by Hindustan Aeronautics. By mid-

Above: Jaguar fighter-bombers of the French Air Force close in for refuelling by Boeing C141 tanker aircraft. Below: Jaguar Internationals awaiting delivery to the Indian Air Force at British Aerospaces Warton facility. Over 80 Jaguar Internationals have been sold abroad, providing revenue for both British Aerospace in the UK and France's Dassault-Breguet company.

Above: The Jaguar E version, the two-seat Advanced and Operational Conversion trainer, which also has a secondary tactical strike and ground attack capability, in service with the French air force. Below right: A Puma helicopter airlifting a 105 mm light gun during exercises on Salisbury Plain.

1984, Jaguar sales worldwide had reached 573, a figure which has since increased with an order for 18 examples placed by the Nigerian air force during 1983.

The described Westland/Aerospatiale agreement of 1976 covered three helicopter types, the French-designed Gazelle and Puma together with the British originated Lynx. The five seat Gazelle utility helicopter first flew during April 1967 and has gone on to become a major export success with examples being operated by the militaries of Egypt, France, Iraq, Jordan, the Lebanon, Libya, Morocco, Quatar, Senegal, Syria, the UK (all three services) and Yugoslavia (who produce it under licence). The 20 seat Puma transport helicopter preceeded the Gazelle with a first flight date of 15 April 1965 and has been even more successful on the world market with examples having been supplied to no less than 35 countries as well as to the French and British armed services.

The British element of this programme, the multi-role Lynx, appeared during 1971 and has had equal success as its French partners in that it has been supplied to Argentina, Belgium, Denmark, West Germany, the Netherlands, Norway and Quatar as well as to the armed services of Britain and France. On the surface,

Top: The successful Westland/Aerospatiale SA-341F Gazelle lightweight helicopter. Above: Joint-manufactured Lynx of the British Army, armed with TOW anti-tank missiles. The Lynx has been exported in both army and naval versions to a number of countries by its Franco-British manufacturers. Left: Puma 20 seat personnel transport carrying troops during an excercise – the product of an Anglo-French consortium.

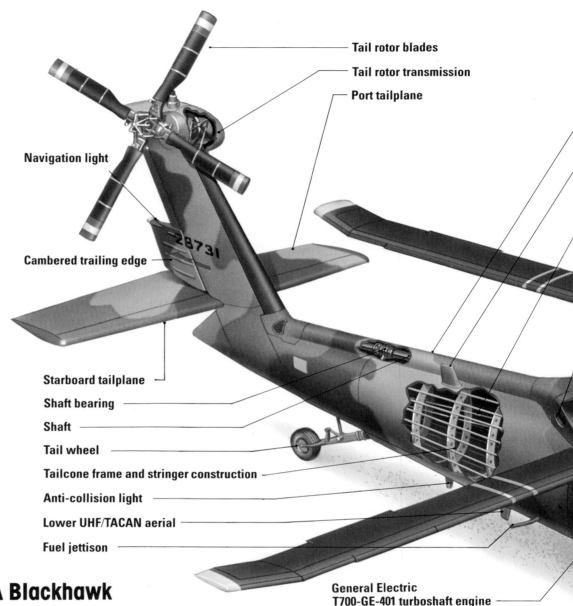

Tail rotor blades

Tail rotor transmission

Port tailplane

Navigation light

Cambered trailing edge

Starboard tailplane

Shaft bearing

Shaft

Tail wheel

Tailcone frame and stringer construction

Anti-collision light

Lower UHF/TACAN aerial

Fuel jettison

General Electric
T700-GE-401 turboshaft engine

Sikorsky UH-60A Blackhawk Helicopter

The one that got away? At the heart of the Westland controversy is this rugged, multi-mission helicopter designed and built by the American company, Sikorsky. For it should have been the next in a line of aircraft initially developed by them and subsequently adapted by British-owned Westlands – predecessors include the Whirlwind, Wessex and Sea King developed from the H-19, S-58 and S-61 respectively. While the US company was actively seeking to create a European market through its customary UK/Westland route, the Ministry of Defence under Secretary Michael Heseltine had already decided to reject the aircraft for its forces, concentrating instead on the joint evolution of a family of 'Eurocopters' with European partners. In this respect, Westland can bring a specialist knowledge of design and manufacture of high quality rotor heads and blades.

With the Sikorsky rescue of the financially troubled Westland group, it was again thought possible a deal could survive – however the MOD remained adamant: The UH-60 as above does not fulfil the requirements it seeks. Designed primarily as a troop and equipment-carrying assault helicopter, Blackhawk also has configurations for tank-busting, light-artillery lifting, reconnaissance, medical evacuation, and search/rescue missions.

Technical Data (gross-weight)

Maximum speed (4000 ft)	146-160 kts
Vertical climb rate (4000 ft)	547 fpm
Service ceiling	19,300 ft
Mission weight	16,293 lbs
Max load weight	20,250 lbs

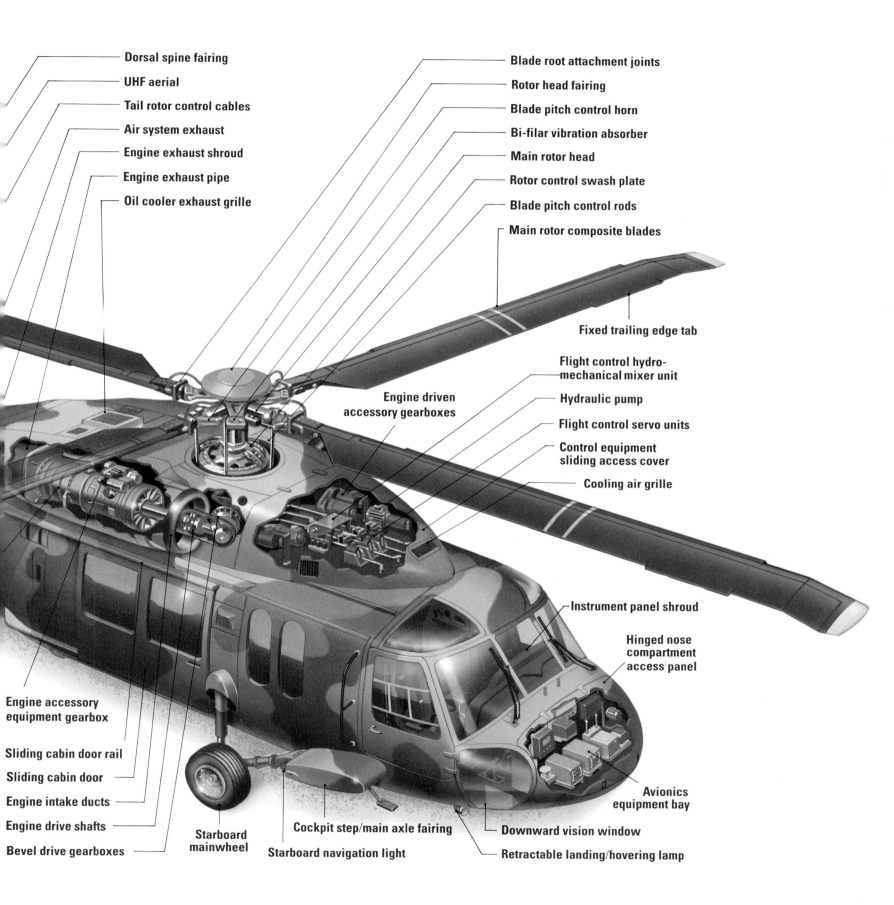

Dorsal spine fairing

UHF aerial

Tail rotor control cables

Air system exhaust

Engine exhaust shroud

Engine exhaust pipe

Oil cooler exhaust grille

Blade root attachment joints

Rotor head fairing

Blade pitch control horn

Bi-filar vibration absorber

Main rotor head

Rotor control swash plate

Blade pitch control rods

Main rotor composite blades

Fixed trailing edge tab

Engine driven accessory gearboxes

Flight control hydro-mechanical mixer unit

Hydraulic pump

Flight control servo units

Control equipment sliding access cover

Cooling air grille

Instrument panel shroud

Hinged nose compartment access panel

Engine accessory equipment gearbox

Sliding cabin door rail

Sliding cabin door

Engine intake ducts

Engine drive shafts

Bevel drive gearboxes

Starboard mainwheel

Cockpit step/main axle fairing

Starboard navigation light

Downward vision window

Avionics equipment bay

Retractable landing/hovering lamp

these initial Anglo-French projects appear to have been very successful and whilst there is no doubt that there is considerable truth in this assertion, they have a darker side. In the case of the Jaguar, it proved very difficult to establish a common specification between the French and British authorities. Equally, there was more than a suspicion that the French co-operated at all because they were in the driving seat in that the Jaguar was based on a French design. Again, the original project also envisaged a carrier-borne variant which was eventually turned down by the French Navy much to the annoyance of the British end of the partnership. Finally, there was further suspicion about whether or not the French were fully committed to the various programmes, a suspicion which seems to be borne out by France's consistently lower orders for the types involved.

Westland experience of European co-operation

If such factors were manifestations of the traditional Anglo-French rivalries and mistrusts, France's relative lack of interest in the naval Lynx certainly set Westland against any future co-operation with the country. This goes a long way towards explaining the company's present stand on the merits of the US-Italian rescue package and that offered by the European consortium.

Westland has had a long standing relationship with Sikorsky stretching back over the Whirlwind, Wessex and Sea King helicopters, all of which were based on Sikorsky designs. Indeed, it is not inaccurate to pinpoint the start of Westland's troubles to the parting of the ways between the two companies over Westland's WG.30. Based on the Lynx, the WG.30 was designed to fulfill the British Air Staff Target 404 for a battlefield transport and with more than an eye to future European requirements as enshrined in the 1978 understanding on a range of military helicopters to be developed and produced in Europe. The sad story of the WG.30's failure in the face of the Ministry of Defence repeatedly 'shifting the goal posts' on the AST 404 specification and then putting its weight behind the European NH 90 requirement and the debacle over an order from India which foolishly led the company to build aeroplanes before the ink was dry on the contract, does not bear repeating in detail. Suffice it to say that Westland was left with an empty order book until the late Eighties and the prospect of going into receivership. At this point, the 'Westland Affair' began.

Below: Westland WG30 Utility Helicopter developed as a private venture by the company. Sales of the type in its military configuration remained disappointing by late 1986, a time of change in Company direction.

Panavia success story

The knotty problems inherent in trying to establish a common specification for a multi-national warplane were triumphantly overcome in Europe's next essay into the co-operative field, the Panavia Tornado. Formed on 26 March 1969, the Panavia consortium is made-up of British Aerospace for the UK, MBB for Germany and Aeritalia for Italy and has gone on to design, develop and produce the Tornado twin-engined all-weather multi-purpose combat aircraft for service with the three national air forces. Described as being "one of the largest European industrial programmes ever undertaken", the Multi Role Combat Aircraft, as the Tornado was initially known, had to fulfill no less than six major requirements in the one airframe, namely close air support/battlefield interdiction, interdiction/counter air strike, air superiority, interception/air defence, naval strike and reconnaissance. Such a multiplicity of requirements was not easy to achieve but the potential of the consortium's work was recognised in July 1976 when the three sponsoring governments signed a Memorandum of Understanding for the production of 809 airframes.

When the first prototype (built by MBB) emerged for its maiden flight on 14 August 1974, the MRCA/Tornado had evolved into a compact, high technology weapons system. With an overall length of 54ft 10in (16.72m), the new aeroplane was externally characterised by a massive vertical tail surface and variable geometry wing surfaces. These 'swing' wings were employed to maximise the aircraft's performance at all

Top: RAF Tornado GR1s from 31 Squadron based at Bruggen, West Germany. These aircraft will eventually take over the role performed by ground-attack Jaguars.
Above: 2 RAF Tornados from the Tri-National Training Establishment at Cottesmore.

points in its flight with maximum sweep being employed at high speeds and minimum when maximum wing surface was needed to generate lift for take-off and landing. Power was provided by a pair of Turbo-Union (itself a multi-national consortium comprising Rolls-Royce (UK), MTU (Germany) and Fiat (Italy)) RB199 afterburning turbofan engines, giving the aircraft a maximum level speed of between Mach 0.92 and 2.2 dependent on the quantity of external stores carried.

Internally, the Tornado houses a complex nav/attack system featuring a nose mounted attack/ground mapping radar, a terrain avoidance system, a Doppler navigation radar system, an inertial navigation system and other high technology features designed to get the aircraft to its target through the worst of Europe's weather at low level. To meet the anticipated defensive threats, the aeroplane features an extensive range of electronic counter measures (ECM) systems designed to both warn the crew of threats and to counter them electronically.

Out of the total order for the type, the RAF is to receive 385 of which 220 will be of the GR Mk 1 interdiction/strike (IDS) model and 165 of the F Mk 2 air defence (ADV) variant. Squadron deliveries of the GR 1 to the RAF began on 1 June 1982 and the service will eventually muster seven strike squadrons and one reconnaissance squadron equipped with the type. The F Mk 2 air defence model is a UK only variant which made its first flight in October 1979 and which was first delivered to the RAF during late 1984. Both the West German air force and naval air arm are to be equipped with the IDS Tornado, German orders for the type totalling 212 for the air force and 112 for the navy. Deliveries to the Luftwaffe began in February 1982 and the service will eventually have four attack groups and a training squadron equipped with the type. The country's navy received its first example in June 1982 and will equip two anti-shipping groups with the type. Most recently, the West German government has authorised development of an electronic warfare derivative of the airframe for service with the Luftwaffe in the early 1990s.

The remaining member of the consortium, Italy has ordered 100 examples of the IDS model which will serve with three operational squadrons of its air force as well as in the training role (12 aircraft). In service, the Tornado has proved itself an excellent combat aircraft which has won major bombing competitions in America during 1984/85. On the export front, orders have been secured for a mixed batch (IDS and ADV models) for Saudia Arabia and there is every likelihood of the type being adopted by both Oman and Jordan.

Tornado project leads to dead end?

The success of the Tornado project might have been expected to open an era of fruitful co-operation between the European nations but not a bit of it. During the late Seventies, it became obvious that a number of European air forces would be looking for a new fighter aircraft to replace their existing equipment at about the same time in the late 1980s/early 1990s. In view of the success of the Tornado, it seemed sensible to see if a similar programme could be undertaken to produce a 'Euro' fighter. In December 1983, the air staffs of France, West Germany, Italy, Spain and the UK issued an outline staff target for such an aircraft with a service entry date in the mid-1990s. A requirement for some 800 'Euro' fighters was anticipated configured primarily for air defence but with a strong secondary capability for ground attack duties. Nationally, the overall figure was expected to break down into 200 examples for France, 250 for Germany, 100 each for Italy and Spain and between 150 and 200 for the UK.

Trouble with the project began with the fact that two of the proposed partners in the project, Britain and France, were already developing aircraft which could form the basis of the new 'Euro' Fighter. As soon as it became clear that the European Fighter Aircraft (EFA) would go ahead, Dassault-Breguet in France was galvanised into action to produce a technology demonstrator in order that it might secure its position in any consortium which might be created. In Britain, building on the experience with the Tornado, British Aerospace had been collaborating with its Panavia partner MBB on just such an aeroplane throughout the Eighties to meet the German TFK 90 and the British AST 414 requirements. As a result of this work, British Aerospace went ahead with its own demonstrator, the Agile Combat Aircraft (ACA), which appeared in mock-up form at the 1982 Farnborough Air Show.

Dassault's demonstrator, the ACX Rafale, was announced at the 1983 Paris Air Show, an announcement which appears to have given the West German government second thoughts about involvement in the British ACA project with the result that MBB withdrew from it. Such a decision was music to French ears as Dassault was seriously worried that it might not be allowed to join any collaborative project if it was based on the ACA.

The remaining Panavia partner, Italy, convinced of the wisdom of collaborative ventures filled the hole left by MBB in the ACA project and has made a major contribution towards it based on the wing design to be used.

The described 1983 agreement was an attempt to pull all the tangled strands together where Britain and Italy were building an aircraft almost identical to that hurriedly produced by Dassault and which was definitely wanted by Germany with the possibility of a Spanish interest! Dassault had indeed played its trump card in producing the Rafale design because the configuration

Above Right: Rollout of the British EAP demonstrator from its assembly hanger at British Aerospace, Warton. Technologies developed for this prototype should prove useful in the production of the Eurofighter. Below: France's answer to the EFA is the Rafale, here seen at its first public unveiling at the Istres test-centre in France.

most suitable for the EFA was a delta wing format with canard foreplanes for manouevrability. This being the case, Dassault announced that its participation in any collaborative project would depend on it being given project leadership in view of its "unquestioned leadership in delta wing fighter design". British Aerospace was having none of it and throughout 1983/84 attempts to break the deadlock continued. The French moderated their demands slightly to a 25% share of the workload and project leadership and when this would not work, weighed in with the fact that France wanted the aircraft for its navy and the British design was too big for such a role.

European split

Such silliness could not go on for ever and in mid-1985, Italy, West Germany and Italy decided to go it alone without the French. This decision somewhat surprised Dassault and resulted in a furious round of further negotiations with the EFA consortium wooing Spain and the French wooing anybody who was interested in the Rafale. The story took an interesting twist when France announced its interest in obtaining a small share in the EFA project whilst still continuing with its own aircraft. Thus, Europe appears to be in the ludicrous position of building two almost identical aircraft intended for the same role in competition with one another. At the present time, Spain has opted to join the EFA consortium and France is busily engaged in developing its own programme, possibly in conjunction with Holland, Denmark, Belgium and Norway who are looking for an F-16 replacement in the same general time scale.

From the foregoing, the reader could be forgiven for seeing collaboration on military aircraft as a peculiarly European concept and one which is bedevilled by French obdurateness. This is not at all the case (nor is France the only culprit in the European arena with Britain showing its own stupidity in this direction by all but pulling out of both the highly successful European Space Launcher programme and the Airbus project) and it is worth rounding off this survey with an overview of what the rest of the world is doing in this direction.

Staying with the European theme for a moment longer, Westland and Agusta have formed EH Industries to produce the EH-101 multi-role helicopter for the British and Italian navies in the early 1990s whilst MBB and Aerospatiale have created Eurocopter to produce the HAP/PAH-2/HAC-3G family of battlefield attack helicopters for use by the French and German armies. Attempts to bring their requirements into line with those of Italy (who independently has produced the A.129 type) and Britain are being made but in view of Westland's preference for an American link up and the

Models of the various configurations for the Eurocopter family of attack and transport helicopters for the 1990s. Top: The French army's escort and support version, known as HAP. Centre: PAH-2 second generation anti-tank helicopter for the German army. Below: The HAC3 French Anti-tank variant.

difficulties over the EFA project, such an arrangement seems increasingly unlikely.

Beyond Europe

Outside the 'European Cockpit', Britain and America are collaborating on the AV-8B development of the successful Harrier VTOL strike aircraft. Up until 1975, this was collaboration of equal partners involving British Aerospace and McDonnell Douglas but in March of that year, the British government opted out of a joint development programme and handed VTOL development on a plate to the Americans. McDonnell Douglas and British Aerospace went ahead separately with developments of the basic Harrier design (including, on the British side, it is reported, a supersonic Harrier) and in 1978, the Americans flew a prototype of a derivative offering increased payload and radius over the existing models. Work on a similar 'big wing' Harrier was undertaken in Britain but was dropped when it became apparent that it would be cheaper to buy into the American AV-8B programme than continue with national developments. Thus, the RAF will receive 60 AV-8Bs under the designation Harrier Mk 5 and design leadership of the Harrier programme will have irrevocably passed into American hands.

A happier opportunity for the British aerospace industry has come about through its involvement in the Swedish JAS 39 Grippen programme. Somewhat similar in concept to the EFA, the nationally produced Grippen

Above: European co-operation in aircraft production to rival the American giants is represented here in the Airbus Industries A310. Below: Mock-up of the Agusta A129 Mangusta anti-tank Helicopter for the Italian Army. Serious interest has been shown by the British in working with the Italians on a joint version of the second generation of this type, a potential counterpart to the US-built Hueycobra.

Top: Following the successful introduction of VSTOL into the US Marine Corps inventory, AV-8B work has begun on the subsequent B version aimed at the development of a supersonic variant of the type. Left: The AV-8 production line at McDonnell Douglas in St. Louis. Above: Artist's impression of the Saab Gripen JAS 39 fighter under development for Swedish Air Force requirements in the 1990s.

Right: The AMX interdiction and close air support aircraft developed by the Italian firms of Aermacchi and Aeritalia and Brazilian aircraft manufacture Embraer. Centre: Yugoslav Air Force IAR 39 at the Paris Air Show. Bottom: Mock-up of the Lavi Multi-Purpose Attack Aircraft under development by Israel Aircraft Industries.

is using British expertise in the production of its wings (indeed British Aerospace is building those to be used on the prototype), a British cockpit environmental control system and avionics and a partly British attack radar. Similar extra national imputs are being given to Israel's Lavi fighter programme which relies heavily on American money and technology. Whilst a wholly national concept, the American Grumman company has designed the aircraft's wings and are supplying the first 50 sets for the production run and the number of American contractors involved in the project reads, in the words of one well known commentator, "like a who's who of the US (aerospace) industry".

The potential for collaboration between the technologically advanced North and the Third World has not gone unnoticed as exemplified by the Italian-Brazilian AM-X close support aircraft. Originating in Aeritalia's AMI project of 1977 for the Italian air force and the joint Macchi-EMBRAER A-X programme for the Brazilian service, the AM-X coalesced as a joint project in 1980 with a work sharing agreement between Aeritalia (46%), Aeromacchi (24%) and EMBRAER (30%). Prototypes of the design are already flying and the type is expected to enter service in the latter half of 1986.

As a final illustration, it is worth noting that multinational collaboration in the development of warplanes is not only a free world phenomen as evidenced by the Roumanian-Yugoslav Yurom programme. Designed to serve the same purposes as the earlier described Jaguar, design work on the Yurom project began in 1970 and resulted in the building of prototypes in both Roumania (the work being done by CNIAR) and Yugoslavia (SOKO) during 1972. Simultaneous first flights were made in both countries on 31 October 1974 and the type has entered service with the air forces of both countries, being known as the IAR-39 in Roumania and as the Oroa (Eagle) in Yugoslavia.

Collaboration here to stay

From the foregoing, it is hopefully clear that collaboration in the development and production of combat aircraft is a well established if sometimes painful concept. Whatever else might be said about Michael Heseltine's resignation over Westland, future historians may well judge him favourably as one of the first British politicians to make a stand over the country's attitude towards Europe and its position in that community of nations. If we must continue to build arms and not be impoverished by their cost, then collaboration is the only sensible way forward. Even more encouraging must be the trust and understanding developed by such ventures which will do so much to break down traditional barriers. Equally, if nations can build arms together, just think what technological collaboration could do in other fields which would benefit man rather than kill him. As one Israeli electronics engineer commented, "if only we had peace, think what our knowledge could do for this land. . . ."

Chapter 7

FUTURE TRENDS: ELECTRONIC BATTLEFIELD

Nowhere has the explosion of technology and the Silicon Valley revolution had more profound effect than in the military. Today's soldier is as likely to be a computer programmer as a sniper, an electronics engineer as a tank driver – and every bit as deadly. Indeed he is probably both.

Interior of the E3A Sentry AWACs aircraft.

There is an undoubted relationship between technological advancement and warfare. This relationship has remained true throughout mankind's history and has changed only in the speed of the advance. The technology of war has reached its apogee in relatively recent times, positively exploding from 1939 onwards. If the reader cares to study the seven years of conflict which began in 1939, he will see enormous strides in weapons capability, technological innovation and sheer killing power compressed into the period. By the end of hostilities, the jet aircraft had both been developed and introduced into combat as had air-to-surface missiles. Again, the ability of a nation to defend itself against aerial attack had been revolutionised by the introduction of radar and the ultimate weapon, the atomic bomb, had proved to be a practical proposition.

Whilst the development of the 'bomb' has probably imprinted itself the most on the public consciousness, it is arguable that the developments in electronics have had the greatest impact on the conduct of warfare. As noted, the appearance of radar revolutionised aerial warfare but this manifestation of the technology is but the tip of the iceberg. The years of World War II saw electronics pervade every aspect of war, providing undreamt of sensory capabilities for the world's air forces and navies, navigational systems of remarkable accuracy, control systems for both existing and newly developed weapons, world wide communications links and the beginnings of computation more powerful than had ever been imagined possible.

If the years 1939-1945 gave life to the technology, then the development of the integrated circuit and the switch from analogue (that is, systems which continuously process data by means of mechanical or electrical 'anologies' such as changes in voltage) to digital (systems which process information in the forms of parcels of numbers, characters or symbols) in computing during the late Sixties and early Seventies has seen it come of age. Today, systems which a mere twenty years ago would have been room sized can be housed in a suitcase as a result of these developments whilst the complexity of problems which can be handled has expanded almost to infinity. Indeed, it is no exaggeration to maintain that warfare is now totally dominated by the concept of the 'electronic battlefield'.

Concentration in W. Germany

To illustrate this concept, we need look no further than the plains of West Germany to see it in action. Here, conventional wisdom has it, is where the Third World War if it ever breaks out will be decided. Accordingly, both the NATO and Warsaw Pact alliances have deployed the greatest concentration of technologically advanced weapons ever seen in a single theatre of war. NATO for its part accepts that in a conventional conflict it will be numerically outnumbered and has accordingly tried to redress the balance by maintaining a technological superiority, the philosophy of making 'every bullet count'. In recent years, this superiority has become increasingly difficult to maintain, leaving the Alliance in a most difficult position. Soviet advances in tactical nuclear delivery systems has made NATO's policy of 'graduated response' – put simply, using nuclear weapons to stop a conventional Soviet advance if all else fails – increasingly suspect. To try and get round the increasing likelihood of a nuclear Armageddon in Western Europe, NATO is once again looking to technology for salvation with many of its commanders pressing for the introduction of high technology conventional weapons systems capable of making a Warsaw Pact thrust into Western Europe prohibitively expensive without having to resort to the nuclear option. Such a policy must be more expensive than the present 'nuclear tripwire' and its cost puts the concept in doubt bearing in mind the present and foreseeable economic climate within the Alliance. Which ever way the argument goes, there can be no doubt that the complexity of the existing weapons systems and their integration into a unified and viable battle plan, let alone the introduction of the 'high tech' systems now being discussed, can only increase the importance of technological battlefield management techniques within NATO. Such an emphasis only serves to heighten the importance of electronic systems which form the basis of such techniques.

Whilst the battlefield of the Twenty First Century will utilise weapons of unparalleled complexity, accuracy and killing power, the basic philosophies of warfare remain materially similar to those established during World War II. Any future conventional conflict in Europe will still be fought with armoured vehicles supported by airpower and the traditional needs of a field commander for good communications, logistics and intelligence will still be primary requirements. What will change progressively is the way in which these requirements are met.

Ptarmigan and Clansman

Taking these elements in order, present and future battlefield communications rely almost solely on electronic means, that is radio and telephonic systems. A current illustration of such a system is the British Army of the Rhine's Ptarmigan battlefield trunk communications system and its integrated family of Clansman equipments. Ptarmigan is intended to be the main conduit for carrying tactical command, administration and logistic information from the Corps commander to the various units under his control. As might be imagined, such a system is highly complex and multi-functional, being capable of being patched into both telephone systems and radio nets and of handling a variety of message formats ranging from voice contact to data transmission.

Overall, Ptarmigan consists of a network of switching 'nodes' interconnected by radio relays. Working from the top downwards, the Corps HQ interfaces into the system by means of the 'nodes' which are positioned at approximately 15.5ml (25km) intervals throughout the

Above: The operator control position in a Parmigan Trunk Switch, part of the cellular system developed for the British Army's most up-to-date communications network. However, Parmigan recently failed to secure a substantial US order.

Corps area. At Divisional level, specialised HQ/access stations both receive orders from above and disseminate information downwards. The Divisional HQs are supported within the system by both the 'switching nodes' and 'radio centrals' which communicate with radio subscribers within a 9ml (15km) radius. Such subscribers are usually made up of mobile units and the system is completed by HQ/task force stations which interface directly with the front line as well as with the higher echelons via the described 'switching nodes' and 'radio centrals'.

Ptarmigan is fairly obviously computer controlled in view of the data transfer permutations necessary to the function of an Army Corps and is compatible with European telecommunications standards so that it can utilise the available civilian systems in time of war and can interface with other European military systems. Historically, Ptarmigan was developed as a result of feasibility studies and trials carried out by the British MOD, the Royal Signals and Radar Establishment at Malvern in

the UK, the British Army School of Signals and the national electronics industry during the Sixties and early Seventies.

Prototype equipment for the Ptarmigan system was completed in 1978 and in 1980, Plessey was awarded a £150 million contract covering an initial four-year production phase which included the delivery of 48 mobile exchanges for use on both soft-skinned and armoured platforms and interconnected by radio relay equipment. This latter item was covered by an ancilliary contract valued at £12 million for 400 Triffid units. Ptarmigan is now in service with the British Army and was a recent contestant in the competition for the supply of such equipment to the US Army, losing out to the similar but considerably cheaper French RITA 'automatic integrated transmission' system.

Clansman tried in Falklands

Supporting this 'strategic' tier of communications, the British Army also employs a supporting 'integrated communications system', the Clansman family of radio equipments. Development of the Clansman family began in the mid-60s and operational units were introduced into service during the early 70s. As a whole, the range covers most military radio needs from man portable units up to fixed vehicular installations with each individual equipment being compatible with the others in the family and suitable for use throughout the world. Currently, the Clansman range is believed to comprise the following elements:–

UK/PRC320
A light weight man portable MF radio operating in the 2-30MHz frequency band and described as being especially suited to long-range patrol/special forces usage.

UK/VRC321 and VRC322
HF radios operating in the 1.5-30MHz frequency band and designed for use in all types of logistic and

Right: Clansman communications system installed in a British Armoured Fighting Vehicle. The system has been continually revised and updated to maintain its effectiveness. Below: The Callpac PRC200 micro processor-controlled High Frequency radio.

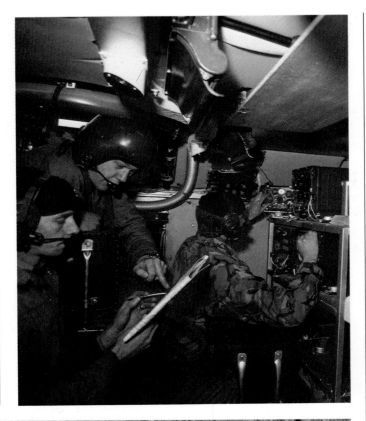

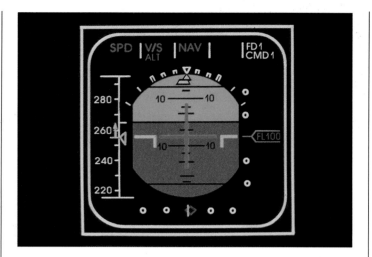

Left: The Plessey Plasma Terminal consists of a display head, a microprocessor control assembly and a keyboard. The display can present text, symbols and simple graphics. Above: High-quality graphics provided by the Quantel Military Paint Box Display.

armoured vehicles. The VRC322 is believed to differ from the VRC321 in having a telegraphic capability.

UK/PRC344
A light weight man portable UHF radio operating in the 225-399.95MHz frequency band.

UK/PRC349
A VHF squad radio operating in the 30-76MHz frequency band.

UK/PRC350
A VHF manpack radio operating in the 36-57MHz frequency band.

UK/PRC351 and PRC352
VHF manpack radios operating in the 30-76MHz frequency band. PRC352 differs from PRC351 in having an additional 20 Watt amplifier to increase power output.

UK/VRC353
A VHF radio operating in the 30-75.975MHz frequency band and designed primarily for use in armoured fighting vehicles.

In service, the Clansman family of equipments have proved to be rugged and dependable items which stood up well to the rigours of combat in the hostile environment of the Falkland Islands during the 1982 South Atlantic campaign.

Such a complex and multi-faceted system as described above constitutes a major element of what is now known as a C3I system, with the acronym standing for 'command, control, communication and intelligence'. C3I nets are now an accepted part of the military structure and are considered vital to successful prosecution of modern warfare. As we have seen in the described Ptarmigan system, computer control is an important element in their function handling the necessary message switching operations, message storage and direction as well as channel selection and integration. This is not however the only role for the military computer on the electronic battlefield. Indeed, there can hardly be a modern battle tank or artillery battery in the European theatre which does not have access to a computer based fire control system. Equally, the nightmarish task of providing a modern army with food, fuel, ammunition and spares (its 'logistic' lifeline) is increasingly relying on computer control to ensure that the right equipment is in the right place at the right time. Again, the computer is playing a vital role in intelligence gathering and as a training aid in wargames. The amount of intelligence data available to the modern field commander has increased enormously over the years since 1945 as a result of advances in sensor technology and a better understanding of how to maximise the potential of an integrated 'all-assets' intelligence gathering operation which uses ground-based, airborne and even space-borne collection platforms. With increasing amounts of data available, computer processing becomes the only viable handling option in an environment in which speed is of the essence. The computer also has a role in the transmission of such data to the units in the front line where there is a need not only for verbal reports but for up-dated maps, graphics of enemy dispositions and even video material relating to the battle area. The UK company Micro Consultants/Quantel has taken this process a stage further and is marketing a computer based system, the 'Military Paint Box', which is designed to quickly and efficiently create the necessary graphic material for the visual presentation of intelligence, briefing or training material.

The satellite factor
Modern C3I systems are rounded out by a further facility, satellite communication links. In the European theatre, such links are not so important to the British Army but are vital to, say, the American forces stationed in the region who have to have secure links with

119

both NATO's command structure in Europe and with the national structure many thousands of miles away in the continental United States. To this end, the Americans have inagurated the 'NATO' satellite programme to handle communications between the US and 13 other countries. The first such satellites, NATO-1 and -2, were launched in March 1970 and February 1971 respectively and stationed 3,697 mls (5,950km) apart, covered the northern hemisphere from Turkey to Virginia in the home country. Ford Aerospace received a contract worth $27.7 million in 1973 for a further three such satellites. The first of these, NATO-3A, was launched in April 1976 and is stationed over the middle of the Atlantic. NATO-3B followed in January 1977 and positioned over the Pacific off America's West Coast is believed to be no longer active. The remaining example in this series, NATO-3C, was placed in orbit during January 1977 and is, like 3A, positioned over the Atlantic, acting as a back-up in case of failures in the existing satellites.

Whilst such electronically based C3I systems 'oil the wheels' of the complex organism which constitutes a modern army, they have a darker side in that they are very vulnerable to interference. Concentrating on the radio elements of such systems, transmissions in the radio part of the electromagnetic spectrum can, by their nature, be readily intercepted by appropriate hostile receiving systems, thereby offering excellent opportunities for intelligence gathering. Such unauthorised 'evesdropping' is not restricted to voice or data transmissions, but is increasingly directed towards the emissions from weapons systems such as the radars associ-

Above: Artist's impression of NATO 3C communications satellite. Right: USAF Block 5D-2 Meteorological Satellite. Recent hardening of NATO ground terminals has been undertaken in an attempt to protect against massive EMP (electromagnetic pulse) following a Soviet nuclear attack which can devastate vulnerable electronics.

ated with battlefield surface-to-air missiles. Such systems have distinct electronic 'fingerprints' which can reveal to an enemy their precise role. Such data is used to build what is known as an 'electronic order of battle' which allows an opponent to, say, work out how to mask his movements from an enemy's sensor system or how to route his air support assets so as to avoid concentrations of AA defences quite apart from the obvious intelligence advantage such information offers.

Measures and Countermeasures

Even more dangerous is the technology of 'electronic warfare' which sets out to disrupt and degrade hostile radio and radar systems. Such operations are termed 'jamming' and take many forms ranging from introducing unwanted signals into a radio receiver so that the true transmission is obscured (noise jamming) to providing such systems as fire control radars with false targets (deception jamming) to degrade their ability to deal with genuine threats. In Europe, the Soviet forces are extremely well equipped for this role having realised at a relatively early date NATO's dependence on radio and radar for the efficient functioning of its forces. Accordingly, the Russians have established specialised 'radio-electronic combat' units to wage an electronic warfare campaign in time of war.

Such units are divided into two distinct types, namely the Signals Interception Battalion (SIB) and the Radio-Electronic Combat Battalion (RECB). The SIB functions as an intelligence gathering organisation picking up both intelligence data from the air waves and locating hostile emitters. According to recent estimates, an SIB comprises 433 officers and men and 114 trucks, divided between an HQ company and specialised radio direction finding, radio intercept and radar intercept units. A radio intercept company has an establishment of 97 officers and men and is equipped with 28 SR-50-M receivers covering voice communications in the VHF/UHF frequency bands. The radio direction finding unit is slightly larger with 118 officers and men and has 16 direction finding sets (SR-19-V, 20-V and 25-V) aimed at locating HF and VHF/UHF voice transmitters. The remaining sub-unit, the radar intercept company, is the largest of the three with 123 officers and men operating 15 intercept receivers covering the 50MHz-10GHz band.

The RECB represents the Soviet army's offensive electronic capability and is made up of three radio and one radar jamming companies, the whole having an establishment of 492 officers and men. The radio jamming units each have a strength of 105 officers and men

and operate four intercept receivers, four direction finding receivers and 15 jamming units. The radar company is manned by 93 officers and men and is equipped with 10 intercept/direction finding receivers and 11 jamming units. Both types of Battalion are highly mobile and are backed up by airborne units which operate jamming platforms based on the Mi-4 and Mi-8 helicopters.

Battle of the beams

NATO takes the threat posed by this organisation very seriously. The Soviet Army's electronic warfare capabilities were dramatically demonstrated during the 1968 Warsaw Pact invasion of Czechoslovakia when an 'electronic screen' was erected to mask activity from NATO observers in West Germany. Indeed, the Soviet Union's capabilities in this direction have led some military observers to believe that NATO's C3I systems could be so devastated as to render communications on any future European battlefield to the level existent in 1916! Equally worrying in this quarter is the effect nuclear weapons have on electronic systems. If a European war was to go nuclear, communications equipment would be subjected to what is known as the 'electro-magnetic pulse' effect. EMP, as the effect is generally described, takes the form of an intense outpouring of electro-

Modern Battlefield Weapons

The illustration shows in stylised form some of the elements to be found in today's sophisticated, electronic battlefield.

KEY TO ILLUSTRATION:
1 Satellite control system
2 E3A AWACS airborne warning control
3 A10 anti-tank aircraft
4 MAVERICK TV-guided missile
5 EC130H jamming Command, Control and Communication links
6 F16 deploying ECM pod containing flares and chaff
7 Tornado deploying target-seeking cluster bombs

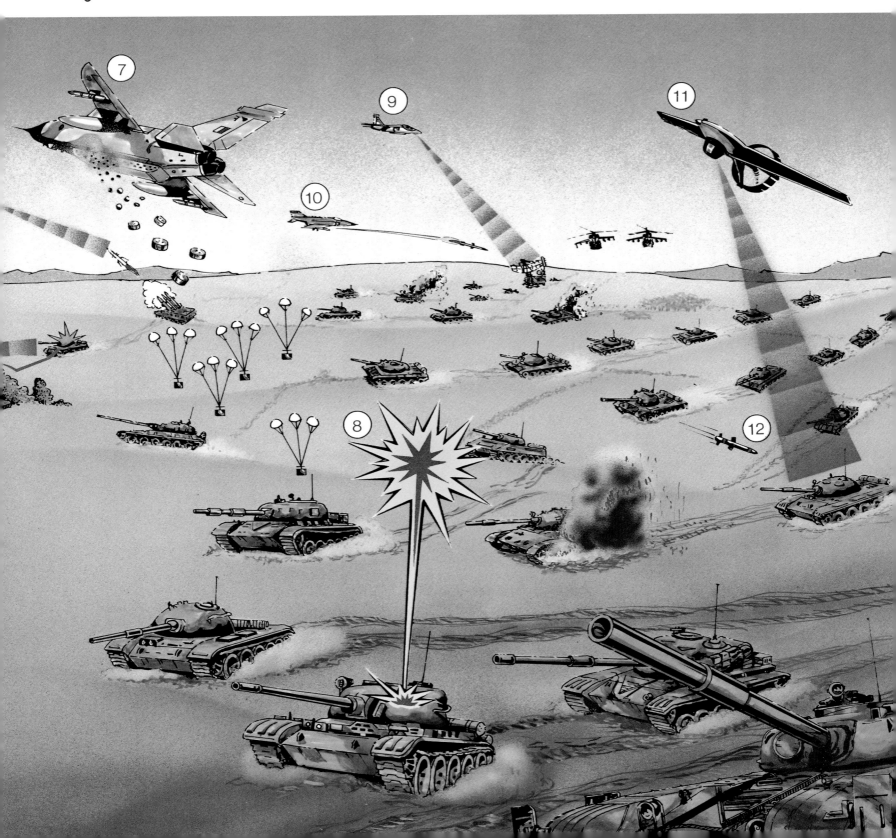

8 Cluster sub-munition detonates shaped
charge upon sensing heat of tank engine
9 EF-11A jamming radar
10 F4G launches HARM missile to destroy Pact
radar
11 Aquilla RPV (remotely piloted vehicle) for
reconnaissance and as shown illuminating
target with laser
12 COPPERHEAD laser guided artillery shell
13 Bell OH-58D scout helicopter illuminates
target with laser

14 AH-64A anti-tank helicopter (from cover)
launches laser guided missiles
15 Challenger tanks
16 Chieftain tanks
17 Leopard 2 tank
18 Control Centre (EW sensors)
19 M110 Self-Propelled Gun

Left: Current systems used for tactical location and jamming of communications include the US Army Teampack system and (right) the AM/MLQ-34 TacJam used in conjunction with Teampack. These may yet be replaced by miniaturised shell-borne systems.

magnetic energy from a nuclear explosion. Such energy has been proved to have a devastating effect on electronic equipment with circuitry overloading and burning out and computer memories being wiped clean. The EMP effect can to an extent be overcome by 'hardening' the particular system against it but such measures are both expensive and contribute to an increase in system size, an important factor for the essentially mobile systems under discussion.

For its part, NATO is also heavily involved in the electronic warfare business. Details of it equipment are less easy to come by for security reasons but can be partially illustrated by considering in outline the US Army's capability in this direction. Within the service, electronic warfare is practiced as both a ground-based and an airborne discipline. On the ground, the capability is concentrated in Military Intelligence Battalions (MIB) which are tasked with Divisional electronic warfare and signals intelligence support. Like its Soviet counterpart, the MIB is multi-functional with separate companies involved in signals interception/emitter location and signals jamming together with a 'guard' function using battlefield radars to give warning of enemy movements. Examples of the equipment used by these formations are the AN/MSQ-103 TEAMPACK signals intercept/direction finding system and the AN/MLQ-34 TACJAM communications jammer. TEAMPACK is a highly mobile system covering the 500MHz-50GHz frequency band which features computer control together with a data link for the onward transmission of received information to a central control and analysis installation.

TACJAM is also a mobile system which employs a number of computer controlled high powered transmitters to generate the jamming combined with a receiver system to identify and establish the parameters of the emitter to be attacked. Currently, it is believed that the US Army has something like 48 TACJAM systems in service or on order. Looking to the future, the Americans are also investigating the potential of what are called 'disposable' jammers for use on the battlefield; that is jammers which are cheap enough and small enough to be emplaced manually or fired in an artillery shell when and as needed. An example of this latter concept is the EXJAM programme which was field tested during 1983/84 and uses a standard 155mm shell as a 'bus' to dispense small jamming transmitters over the battlefield at pre-set intervals during the course of its flight.

Specialised aircraft for ECM role

As might be expected from a service as aware of the potential of aircraft as an aid to ground warfare as the US Army (the world's largest user of military helicopters), increasing use is being made of what are described as 'special electronic mission aircraft' (SEMA) both as intelligence tools and as electronic warfare platforms. Within Europe, the US uses a surprisingly wide range of both fixed wing aircraft and helicopters as

SEMA platforms, including the EH-1H SOTAS helicopter and the RV-1D and RC-12D electronic reconnaissance aircraft. For those unfamiliar with the term, 'electronic reconnaissance' can be defined as intelligence gathering in the electro-magnetic spectrum, that is radio and radar signals. The discipline is also known by the acronym SIGINT which stands for SIGnals INTelligence.

Taking the illustrations in order, the US Army currently operates four radar equipped EH-1H helicopters in Germany as part of the SOTAS (Stand Off Target Acquisition System) programme. As its name suggests, SOTAS is intended to locate hostile movements on the battlefield for targetting purposes. The four EH-1H aircraft carry a large plank shaped radar scanner beneath their fuselages and were to have been replaced by a larger number of SOTAS equipped EH-60B Blackhawk helicopters in the late 80s. The EH-60B flew in prototype form during 1981 but thereafter, the programme ran into cost and technical difficulties and has been abandoned. Whilst the EH-60B will not now enter service, the US Army is currently involved in the JSTARS (Joint Surveillance Target Acquisition Radar System) programme with the USAF to provide wide area battlefield surveillance which in part fulfills the SOTAS requirement. Mounted on a modified Boeing 707 airframe bearing the military designation C-18, JSTARS uses a synthetic aperture radar with a moving target indicator facility. These terms are not as fearsome as they sound, simply indicating that the JSTARS radar uses a technique of multiple readings to produce a single image and is

Top: The Grumman RV-1D Mohawk of the US Army, which carries the Quicklook-3 system which is able to locate hostile radar sites. Above: Pilatus- Britten-Norman's Islander, contender for the Castor concept for battlefield data acquisition.

capable of detecting moving targets. The system is intended to provide information on such things as tank movements and those of battlefield helicopters, with the data being used to orientate artillery and air support responses. The British are also developing a similar system known as CASTOR (Corps Airborne Stand-Off Radar) to support the country's forces in Germany. Two radars have been evaluated in the role and the operational system will most likely be deployed in a modified Canberra aircraft.

equipped with the 'Guardrail' signals intercept and direction finding system aimed at hostile communications links.

Electronic intelligence

From the foregoing, it will be obvious that there is a certain blurring of the distinctions between electronic warfare and the traditional intelligence gathering task. As we have seen, electronic sensors are becoming increasingly important to the latter discipline by way of the need to gather 'orders of battle' for hostile electronic systems as their use multiplies on the battlefield, the importance of intercepted communications and the ability to 'see' in conditions which would defeat the human eye or the camera.

Whilst the use of airborne platforms as a reconnaissance tool over the battlefield has long been understood, the electronic revolution of the 50s and 60s has vastly increased the general capability. As has been noted, radar is becoming an increasingly important battlefield surveillance tool as infra-red detection, using sensors which react to the heat generated by a weapons system or even of a squad of soldiers. Both techniques are very important in that they are relatively unaffected by haze, low light conditions or even darkness. Equally, infra-red sensors can be used to establish the location of camouflaged installations, their state of operational readiness and even where a system has been located prior to a move through examination of the residual heat 'footprints'. So sophisticated is this technique becoming that the Americans have embarked on the 'Teal Ruby' programme which uses satellite based infra-red sensors to track aircraft and missiles over the battlefield. The programme as a whole has suffered a major set-back with the loss of the Space Shuttle *Challenger* but there is little doubt that the programme will eventually be resumed, US forces in Germany already having been geared towards including it as an intelligence source as early as March 1985.

Unmanned aerial observers

Looking to the short term future, there is considerable interest in RPVs (Remotely Piloted Vehicles) for battlefield reconnaissance purposes. Such a use of drones has been pioneered by the Israelis who made experimental use of such platforms during the ill-fated invasion of the Lebanon. Currently both the British and American armies in Europe are looking at such programmes with interest for the former centering on the Phoenix airframe and the latter on MQM-105 Aquila vehicle. Taking these in order, the British Phoenix project is intended to provide a drone platform to complement the described CASTOR radar system in support of the country's forces in Germany. With a predicted service entry date in the late 80s, the Phoenix vehicle will be equipped with an infra-red sensor to generate images which will be transmitted digitally and in 'real time' for analysis. The MQM-105 Aquila will serve a similar func-

Top: Still in the future, but of particular importance to the US Military are the Teal Ruby and J-Stars programmes, currently undergoing research and development. J-Stars is an airborne surveillance system designed to detect and locate enemy ground targets and guide attacking aircraft on to them. Teal Ruby (above) is an experiment in the HALO programme developing a space-based mosaic infra-red array for detecting and tracking air activity over hostile or foreign air space.

Returning to the cited illustrations, the RV-1D aircraft is a derivative of the familiar Mohawk observation aircraft configured to carry the AN/ALQ-133 emitter location system covering the VHF/UHF-18GHz band. Known as 'Quicklook', ALQ-133 is most probably designed to find hostile radar sites and the US Army has a number of RV-1D aircraft already operational in Germany. The RC-12D variant of the Beech Super King Air 200 commuter airliner is also operational in Germany,

tion for the American forces and is intended to undertake missions of three hours duration with a sensory payload made up of low light television and forward looking infra-red equipment. In a combat environment increasingly dominated by radar directed missile and AA gun systems, the use of relatively cheap and relatively expendable drones for reconnaissance purposes must be obvious.

As a final illustration of the marriage of electronic sensors to airborne platforms as battlefield surveillance tools, it is worth noting the USAF's introduction of the TR-1A to the European theatre. Closely related to the later models of the infamous U-2 'spyplane', the TR-1A is designed solely for support of the battlefield rather than the strategic role of its forebears. To this end, the aeroplanes are equipped with an extensive range of highly classified ELINT and COMINT equipment (ELectronic and COMmunications INTelligence equipment aimed at recording, respectively, the electronic signatures of radars and hostile radio communications). In the immediate future, such systems will be augmented by an advanced synthetic aperture surveill-

Easily identified as a high-altitude reconnaissance aircraft by its long, glider-like wings, the Lockheed TR 1a was developed from its infamous predecessor the U.2. for on-the-spot battlefield surveillance and control. Operating altitudes are known to be in excess of 60,000 ft.

ance radar and the PELS (Precision Emitter Location System) system designed to target hostile emitters for attack.

Whilst the subject of the electronic battlefield is worthy of book-sized treatment, it is hoped that the foregoing will have given at least a flavour of the subject in its European context. The importance of the subject cannot be over emphasised as the electronics revolution has pervaded every aspect of the modern soldier's life from the way he is fed and paid, through the function of the weapons he operates to the way his commanders make tactical decisions and communicate their orders to him. Today's combat environment is no place for the technologically illiterate and if it is possible to divine the future of warfare, the dominance of the 'black box' over virtually every other component of warfare can only continue to increase.

Chapter 8

FORCES DIARY: RETRO-SPECTIVE

A glance back at the defence year – budget cuts, political rows, Britain's overseas commitments and where the big contracts go will all have an effect on the immediate future of the military establishment. Forces '87 assesses some of the implications of current defence expenditure.

Ex-defence minister Heseltine, casualty of the Westland saga, talking to Paras before his resignation.

At the time last year's Forces Diary went to press Michael Heseltine, MP, Secretary of State, was very firmly in his cabinet seat. The opening lines of that review likened his task to that of learning to play a violin in public. It appears, with the benefit of hindsight, that this observation was particularly apt, Westlands being the final squeak on the E string that made the said minister politely disengage from further attempts at public harmonising. This said, the management of the nation's defence is seldom one that can be indelibly stamped with the authority of just one person since the political, economic and now increasingly industrial forces at play are too strong to be orchestrated by a single figure, however powerful the office.

Since January 1986, when George Younger took over as Secretary of Defence the three R's of economic necessity, NATO planning and resource optimisation have been essential to the underlying policies and activities of the MOD. And all those concerned with their implementation have generally kept as low a public profile as is possible with a government drawing towards election time. With the electorate knocking on the doorstep the Conservative government has naturally been dressing the MOD establishment for the best possible performance in stringent times. Manpower numbers have been massaged to look as if the they sit on the right rail of the abacus and the BAOR teeth arms are starting to feel the effect of at least five years overall streamlining and equipment augmentation. Meanwhile the commitment

to improving and augmenting the reserve forces for both home defence and frontline purposes continues. Provided the uncertainties of defence spending do not undo the work of gradual improvement over recent years, the period from 1987 to early 1990s should see a consolidation of policies made in the first part of the 1980s. In all respects this has been a very important era in the consolidation of a Western approach, primarily under the aegis of the NATO alliance, so the knock-on effects of present defence planning are going to be crucial. In the early part of the 1980's the commander of 1 (BR) Corps in Germany referred to the decade as 'the window of the Eighties', by which he inferred that if ever there was to be a chance for the Soviet Union and Warsaw Pact to be aggressive, and perhaps an overriding economic need, it is in this decade. Such a feeling generally was very much the premise upon which the strengthening of NATO has been brought about, and is being continually examined.

This review examines the major commitments and some of the important underlying themes of British and NATO military activity that are important to the Forces in 1987 and the near future. The review also gives details of selective activities in terms of recent and projected exercises, events, ceremonies, shows and exhibitions undertaken by the three services.

Below: Defence Secretary George Younger in the cockpit of the £180 million experimental fighter aircraft unveiled in April, described as the best British-designed fighter for 30 years.

The NATO Commitment

The last year has seen a growing debate – often conducted in public – about NATO's strategy of flexible response and the augmenting of forward defence numbers and equipment; about the roles of conventional and nuclear weapons in the European theatre needed to ensure credible deterrence; and the adoption of new technologies required to improve these weapons. Within the NATO defence planning structure the detailed discussion of these issues takes place at a biennial planning process which involves Defence Ministers of all member states participating in an integrated military structure. Resulting from this, every two years Ministers produce highly worked policy guidelines, known as Ministers Guidance, which are issued to major NATO commanders and member nation governments. These 'orders' set out the political, economic, military and technological factors that could effect the development of NATO forces and their impact on NATO strategy.

Ministers Guidance

The last Ministers Guidance was issued in May 1985 and its particular purpose was to cover the medium term period from that date until 1992. In addition to the Guidance another important planning instrument in NATO is the NATO five-year plan which is regularly drawn up in response to a NATO Defence planning questionnaire which records each member nation's progress in the implementation of Force Goals, together with economic, logistic and force level plans. The last Five-Year plan was put into consideration in December 1985 to cover the years 1986 to 1990.

The coordination and implementation of these all-in-one type policy pot boilers is a long-term business. Any initiatives coming from this centralised body politic generally takes a long time to reach executive stage and in the gestation period are refined, studied, given to committee, chewed over and expediently adapted until they are rendered into a swallowable state for each NATO nation to absorb. In the process a tremendous amount of energy is tied up with each member nation jockeying for position, especially where joint contribution budgets are concerned, force roles are examined and high office is appointed.

The Ministerial Guidance of 1985 has several interesting objectives:

- a resolution to sustain NATO's strategy of flexible response and forward defence;
- to maintain the effectiveness of NATO's nuclear forces;
- to improve conventional forces in relation to those of the Warsaw Pact;
- to optimise resources on a cooperative Alliance basis;
- to improve the methodology involved in common funding;
- to cooperate on the use of arms, particularly in resource provisions for strengthening conventional forces;
- improving methods of measuring productivity;

- developing more effective transatlantic arms cooperation;
- sharing the costs of research, development and technology related to arms and equipment within Europe and increasing this area of cooperation between Europe and North American members of the NATO Alliance;
- maintaining and consolidating efforts in the field of arms control.

The extent to which these predominantly hopeful declarations of intent will be forcefully pursued depends largely on the critical issue of defence spending and joint costs which inevitably relate to the strategic benefits each member nation can achieve from NATO policy as a whole. But all NATO member states have been effectively asked to critically review their own financial navels whilst the major deficiencies in each nation's defence effort are being examined on a joint basis.

Long-term planning

NATO supervisors are also heavily involved in the long-term plans, methods and strategies – based on sensible evaluations of present trends that enable the Alliance to look ahead for up to 20 years. NATO military authorities are, for example, devising a Conceptual Military Framework, specifically designed to take into account conventional defence improvements in the light of emerging technology. The Alliance has also set up a Long-Term Planning Guideline on the interdiction of Soviet follow-on forces, sometimes referred to as FOFA. The principal application of FOFA thinking is ways of making NATO capable of checking the overwhelming momentum that conventional Warsaw Pact forces can bring to bear on a particular axis, by using new technology. Of equal importance is holding such forces back and eventually defeating them in the case of such a dire breach. To do this a comprehensive range of modern weaponry would be needed. A great deal of emphasis is consequently already being given to sustaining and improving the frontline by restructuring the divisions into very adaptable Battle Groups and by applying new technology to the battlefield.

The awesome fear behind this philosophy of frontline improvement is based on the current disparity between NATO's conventional forces and those of the Warsaw Pact risking an undue reliance on the early use of nuclear weapons.

Frontline improvements

The reorganisation of 1 (BR) Corps, for example, has resulted in balanced frontline resources and stronger reserves. Within the Corps there are three regular armoured divisions, two of which are deployed forward and are better able to cope with short-warning attack. One of the brigades of the third division has undergone trials in the air-mobile role to improve its capability to deal rapidly with unexpected breakthroughs. Additionally, the incorporation of Challenger and MLRS (see *Forces 86*) and the improved communication technology

Above: The MLRS is scheduled for acquisition by the US, West Germany, Italy, France and Britain through the latter half of this decade. Rocket warheads can be adapted for anti-armour or anti-personnel roles.

for RAF Germany, are helping to tighten frontline defence.

Other new equipments being examined for feasibility include the NATO Frigate Replacement (NFR 90), the Long-Range Stand-Off Missile and a Short-Range Anti-Radiation Missile (SRARM). Wherever there are long term military applications Ministers Guidance has stated the need to cooperate on the development of the technologies involved.

The British Contribution to NATO

The UK contribution to NATO is concentrated into four areas as follows:

British Nuclear Forces It was decided in 1980 that Trident should replace Polaris as an independent national strategic deterrent that would maintain its effectiveness until at least 2020. This decision is the subject of great contention still but is justified by the government primarily because the Trident D5 multi-warhead nuclear armed submarines ensure commonality with the equipment of our most powerful ally from whom it was bought. Trident is also reckoned to be economical because it would enjoy through-life logistic support which would keep running costs down. The system allows each submarine plenty of defensive capability and sea-room.

The United Kingdom Apart from being the Homeland and therefore a prime defence commitment, the UK is an essential base for NATO support. It is a forward base for NATO forces operating in the Eastern Atlantic and North Sea, a main base for Channel operations and a support base for British and American forces stationed on the mainland of Europe as well as for other reinforcements in times of tension or war.

The European Mainland Divided into the two principal regions: The Central Region – the Alliance's Heartland

Above: Acquisition of the latest generation US-built Trident ICBM continues to provoke political and military controversy. Another source of contention has been the BAe Nimrod AEW Aircraft (top right). Radar equipment and VDU screens with keyboards take up much of the interior (right) but the system has yet to prove workable, and remains under threat from the proven US AWACs.

in Europe – and the Northern Region. In the Central region as Force Cmnd 8288 said "The forward defence of the Federal Republic is the defence of Britain itself". We maintain 55,000 troops and a tactical airforce. In wartime the British force will treble with a good deal of imput from the reserve forces. In the Northern Region Britain commits mobile amphibious forces, predominantly in the persons of the Royal Marines, with an airborne capability to help contain Soviet and Northern Baltic Fleets.

The Eastern Atlantic and Channel This area is vital to the defence of the UK and NATO's Northern flank and to the safe passage of reinforcements of equipment,

manpower, and oil crossing the Atlantic. Europe would depend on these resources to succeed in a European conflict. Britain is NATO's major European maritime power and virtually the entire Royal Navy is assigned a NATO task as are a large number of maritime aircraft such as the Nimrod. We also provide permanent contributions to NATO's Standing Naval Force Atlantic and Standing Naval Force Channel.

In all these areas the essentials of British commitments – both in terms of numbers and force capabilities – remain unchanged for the forseeable future.

Collaboration in Europe

There is an inevitable financial and geographical gulf between North American and European NATO allies. As Ministers Guidance has stipulated collaboration on the European side is an essential commitment in the last part of this decade. Where the joint ventures in the research, development, production and commissioning of defence equipment are concerned, there are many advantages: equipment standardisation increases the possibility of interoperations and flexibility of this kind is very much in demand; also the unit cost savings accruing to joint efforts makes it possible to produce and deploy a greater number of equipments.

A brief survey of recent years shows the creditable result of this work: Jaguar, the Anglo-French helicopters, FH70 and Tornado are all the result of joint activity. The table below shows some past and current work in this field (see *Planemakers*).

BRITISH COLLABORATION

Project	Participating countries
1. In Service	
Naval Equipment:	
PARIS Sonar	UK/FR/NL
Land Equipment:	
FH70 Howitzer	UK/GE/IT
Scorpion Reconnaissance Vehicle	UK/BE
Aircraft:	
Jaguar	UK/FR.
Tornado	UK/GE/IT
Lynx	
Gazelle	UK/FR
Puma	
Missiles:	
Martel (Air-to-Surface) UK/FR	
Milan (Anti-Tank)	UK/FR/GE
Sidewinder (Air-to-Air)	UK/GE/IT/NO
Other Equipment:	
Midge Drone UK/CA/GE	

Top: British-built Scorpion Light Tank of the Belgian Army. Above: The Belgians also deploy Spartan APCs. Top right: Jaguar GR1s are operated by France and Great Britain, seen here during a low-level exercise. Right, above: The GR5 Harrier aircraft, developed jointly by Britain and the US. Below right: One of the success stories of European co-operation has been the development and production of Milan, here fitted with MIRA thermal nightsight. Far right: The SP-70 155 mm self-propelled Howitzer developed by Italy, West Germany and Britain.

2. In Development or earlier Study Phases

Project	Participating countries
Naval Equipment:	
NATO Frigate Replacement	UK/US/NL/FR/CA/SP/GE/IT
Sea Gnat Decoy System	UK/DE/US
Land Equipment:	
SP70 Howitzer	UK/GE/IT
Multiple Launch Rocket System Phase I	UK/FR/GE/IT/US
MLRS Phase III	UK/FR/GE/US
Aircraft:	
Harrier GR5	UK/US
Naval ASW Helicopter EH101	UK/IT
European Fighter Aircraft	UK/FR/GE/IT/SP

Project	Participating countries
Missiles:	
Short-Range Anti-Radar Missile	UK/US/BE/GE/CA/IT/NL
Long-Range Stand-Off Missile	UK/US/GE
Milan Improvements	UK/FR/GE
TRIGAT (Anti-Tank)	UK/FR/GE
ASRAAM (Air-to-Air)	UK/GE/NO
Other Equipment:	
Midge-Post Design Services UK/FR/GE	

As the table shows, there is heavy British involvement in these projects – it should be pointed out, however, that the UK will not necessarily participate in the full development and production of all of these equipments.

Beyond NATO

Bearing in mind that within the aegis of NATO are the overseas posts of Cyprus and Gibraltar, Britain still has extensive commitments and security objectives on a wider international basis. These range from Hong Kong, now only ten years from being ceded to the Chinese, with a population of around five million, to the Pitcairn Islands with a population of only 60. To meet these responsibilities we presently maintain garrisons, with a supporting naval presence, in Hong Kong and the Falklands, and have other forces based in the commonwealth countries of Belize and Brunei.

Because exports currently represent about 30 per cent of Britain's gross domestic product, we have a prevailing interest in seeing that peace and stability is maintained in countries constituting our trading partners; also in seeing that there is an unhindered flow of important raw materials such as oil and minerals; and in keeping sea trade routes open in key areas. Consequently, strategic locations and facilities such as Diego Garcia and the Ascension Islands are important to Britain in adding her part to the Western economies' burden in maintaining healthy and fruitful relations in areas around the world that are frequently unstable.

Personnel exchanges

Similarly, we commit naval forces to the Arabian Sea and the Caribbean and pursue a worldwide programme of military deployments and exercises. In 1986, a number of military personnel were posted on exchanges, usually for training evaluation and diplomatic reasons, to American and Canadian military establishments at middle rank officer level. There has also been some exchange with antipodean and Far Eastern countries. Supporting the diplomatic effort in both NATO and other countries military attaches have played an equally significant role in flying the flag – even in Peking. All of this activity is deemed vital to preserving the status quo.

The political pressures and tension at play in many overseas regions are unlikely to be reduced in the forseeable future. Whilst Britain still has an overseas commitment relating to her much-diminished Commonwealth, her part in sharing the complex duty of protecting Western economies' in general has in many ways broadened the overseas defence role. The next few years might see a consolidation of military assistance programmes and those enabling an effective intervention capability.

The greater part of British defence is involved, as mentioned above, in the forward defence of Europe, and the Eastern Atlantic. But of growing importance in recent years has been the consolidation of stronger defence forces based in the UK.

In the role of air defence the main recent contribution

Left: Women at Arms – a 'greenfinch' of the Royal Ulster Constabulary, which began recruiting women in 1973 to help in searches involving women. They are, in fact, unarmed.

has been the Tornado F2 and since late 1984 seven squadrons have been gradually brought into operation although the last two of these will probably not be delivered until 1988. Two squadrons of Phantoms are remaining in service with improvements made to their weapon systems to ensure their potency as air defence aircraft until the early 1990's. Because of the deployment of a Phantom squadron in the Falklands, the American Phantom F4J's were introduced in 1985 to bridge the gap.

Air defence at home

The modernisation of the complex of ground radars and command, control and communications systems for air defence (The United Kingdom Air Defence Ground Environment – better known as UKADGE) is nearing completion this year, although there will be progressive adjustments and further refinements to this important protective system for some years to come. Also helping ground defence, two squadrons of the Rapier Wing have been formed, owned by British-based USAF but operated by the RAF Regiment.

Nimrod AEW problems

At the time of going to print the Nimrod Early Warning (AEW) aircraft was still causing headaches following a series of radar and other equipment trial hiccoughs. The fully operational Nimrod – planned originally to be fact by 1984 – now looks doubtful even for this year. When it does come into operation some technical observers have reckoned that the electronics involved may no longer be state-of-the-art as a result of the gestation period from contract to final commissioning. But whatever this may mean there is no doubt that the new Nimrod will bring a formidable presence into the AEW forum of activities. Perhaps more important is the nature of MOD contracting and policy-tendering and the degree to which joint ventures can be made successful when large private corporations such as British Aerospace and parts of GEC have communication problems (See *Planemakers*).

Vital UK installations

Last year's forces diary reported on the other important area of home defence, that of protecting vital ground bases and priority civil installations. After some revision, the American philosophy of deploying greater numbers of reserve and home defence forces was tested in September 1985 in an exercise called Brave Defender. As a result of this exercise the government has confirmed its commitment to enhance existing reserve forces and create more companies – mostly hosted by the various TA units – in the recently established Home Defence Force. Current recruiting activity is aimed at achieving the manning target of 5000 Home Defence members divided regionally into 43 companies.

Another important activity involving the reserves is the drive to modernise mine countermeasures (MCM)

Above: British Forces abroad serve not only the Crown, but can also be called on to provide part of the UN Security Forces, as here in Cyprus, where an uneasy peace is maintained between Greek and Turkish lines.

capabilities. The Soviet Union poses a serious threat to naval and merchant shipping movements, especially in approaches to the Clyde. The *Ton*-class MCM vessels have long been in service and added to these there are now 11 *Hunt* Class MCM vessels which should come into operation by the end of this year and a total of 12 *River* Class Sweepers for use mainly in training and operation by the Royal Naval Reserve.

A new vessel will be brought into service probably in early 1988, this being the first of the Single Role Minehunters (SRMH). This will be equipped with a new generation of variable-depth mine-hunting sonar to tackle the Soviet Union's most modern sea mines. Plessey have won the contract to develop fully this equipment and MOD are searching for new ways to update the Navy's defensive mining capability (See *Plastic Navy*).

The Cost of Defence

With the exception of the United States, Britain spends

more on defence in absolute terms and per capita than any other ally in NATO. As a statistical fact, however, this information is misleading: we are only marginally ahead of Norway and significantly behind the US in total amount; in terms of Gross National Product the percentage of GNP Britain spends is 5.3 with Greece spending 6.8 and the US in the lead with 6.9

Over the period of the conservative government there has been a significant real growth in defence expenditure, worked out on an Alliance-prescribed basis, of 3 per cent each year between the financial years of 78/79 and 85/86.

Last year, however, was the last one in which this commitment was to be holding, and the MOD has to go back into the fighting arena along with other government departments in order to justify real growth in the latter part of this decade. This means that defence budget managers are faced with the problem of maintaining the initiatives of the first part of the decade and the strengthened capabilities that these initiatives have brought about, whilst not having firmly committed resources to make this a surety. The government's justification for withdrawing a firm commitment is based on the hope that, given the imponderables of technological and industrial restraints and opportunities, flexible approaches to the use of resources will be maintained. In other words some of the projects planned may not come about because of circumstances outside governmental control so the money destined for these projects may be available for other expedient uses. Budget massaging is the necessary evil of all government departments whatever the government in power.

Falklands expenditure

For this financial year (86/87) and FY87/88, spending plans reflect a fall in expenditure in the Falklands. The present government is very keen to 'rationalise' this area of expenditure, unforseen when it came to power.

Given the extra spending on equipment since 1979 (40 per cent of the total Defence Budget), which stood at 46 per cent in FY85/86, and the commitment to increasing the value of this money by establishing greater efficiency, the government hopes that the defence improvements of the past five or so years will be more easily consolidated within renewed budget constraints. The main imponderable in this formula, however, is pressure being applied from the United States. The US currently spend an astronomical 350 billion dollars on defence activity and there is a strong undercurrent of popular indignation amongst US taxpayers at the enormity of this amount which may cause the US senate to demand that other NATO allies share the burden of American initiatives, conceived for the common good.

British budget

In FY85/86 Britain laid down a budget of £18,060 million which is marginally more than the budget for the same year for Education and Science, although a little less

Above: British Territorials taking part in Brave Defender. Their job will be to protect vital installations from behind-the-lines enemy raids. Right, above: 5th Royal Inniskillin Dragoon Guards play the role of attacking Spetsnaz forces during the Home Defence exercise. Below Right: RAOC Bomb Disposaleer in full ceramic anti-blast kit. The increase in terrorism has underlined the need for efficient means of detecting and neutralizing concealed explosives, while trying to protect the defusers.

than half the amount spent on social security. Part of this money has to go on 'non-recurring' capital expenditure for new British equipments in development. These include Sonar 2050, Blue Vixen Radar, Scot Shipborne Satellite Terminals, Harpoon Surface-to-Surface Missiles, Vertical Launch Sea Wolf, Replacement Small Calibre Gun, Weapon Handling and Discharge System for submarines, Phoenix Remotely-Piloted Vehicles. And apart from the enormous costs of paying and training regular and reserve forces, a spot check, at 85/86 prices, of the cost of certain items in the MOD shopping list, makes interesting reading:

A type 23 Frigate costs 110 million
A Harrier GR5 costs 14.2 million
A River Class Minesweeper costs £4.5 million
TACAN Navigational Equipment costs £32,000
A single Milan (A-T) Missile costs £7,500
VHF radio costs £6,000
The Combat High boot costs £20 a pair
Naval Anti-Flash Gear costs £7 per outfit

Regular, reserve and civilian MOD staff cost £6.271 billion in 1986; equipment cost £8.855 billion; and expenditure on MOD works, building and land, as well as miscellaneous stores and services cost £3.433 billion.

The following table shows a little more closely how this is broken down:

	Millions £
Navy general purpose combat forces	2,505
Nuclear Strategic Forces	509
European Theatre Ground Forces	2,764
Other Army Combat Forces (Med., Hong Kong, South Atlantic, other areas)	205
Air Force general purpose forces	3,702
Reserve and Auxiliary formations	360
Research and Development	2,304
Training	1,204
Repair and associated facilities in UK	917
War and contingency stocks	535
Other Support functions	2,998
Miscellaneous expenditure and receipts	34

Gradual manpower cuts

Whilst there is every sign of increased recruitment activity in the reserve sectors of all three services there has been a gradual overall cut back in manpower largely as a result of rationalisation programmes in the various service, support and staff jobs and appointments. The diminishment on a yearly basis is only 0.7 per cent since the beginning of 1985 which is about 2,400 personnel per year out of a present total of about 324,000. The cuts have principally come from the Royal Navy in both the officer and rating ranks – the total numbers in the Royal Navy now being only around 63,000. The RAF saw an increase of 140 officers in 1985 whilst during that year there was a decrease of 133 officers in the Royal Navy. Army strengths remained about the same in the officer ranks but it is interesting to note that at

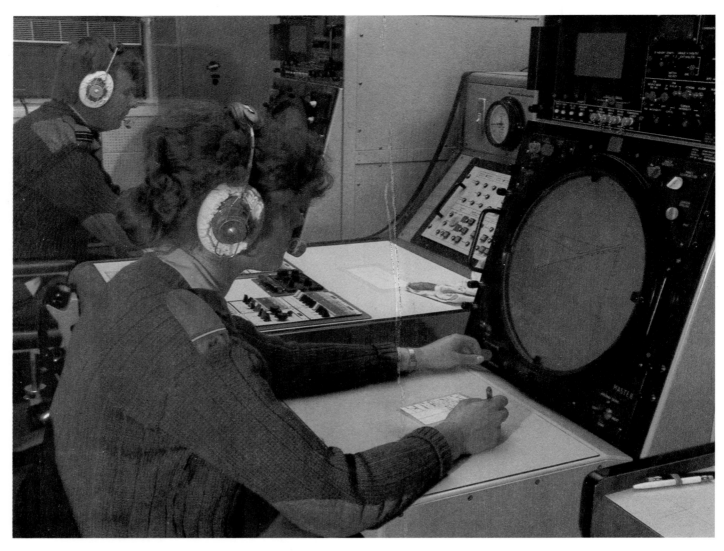

the beginning of 1986 there were 51 more women officers in the Armed Forces and a total of 70 less male officers since the year before. Because of the exceptionally high quality of female officers taken into the Service in all three Services combined with the trend toward optimising the efficiency of the support services, women are generally being used for a greater number of jobs and their relative numbers are increasing despite overall cut backs.

Rationalisation of senior appointments
Recent efficiency studies in higher staff posts have resulted in the rationalisation of a number of senior appointments particularly in central MOD staff jobs. Again, there is a possibility that there will be more women in relatively high positions than was the case five years ago.

The community role
As well as being a separate community within the wider civilian community, the part that all servicemen and women play in the local communities and British society at large, is increasingly important. Every year the Ser-

Above: A Flying Officer in the RAF's Air Traffic Branch talks down a Harrier pilot by radar in bad weather. Britain's air traffic radar network is currently being upgraded with the introduction of improved new equipment and the improved Martello system.

vices put their specialist skills to work in order to supplement or initiate community projects ranging from giving swimming instruction in local schools to helping on National Trust developments, using young people to help build bridges, make footpaths or work on archaeological sites.

In bad weather conditions or times of natural disaster such as forest fires or floods, the Army and RAF are often first to lend a hand providing vehicles, drivers, divers, and even running emergency 'meals on wheels' to outlying districts that sometimes get cut off.

Aid to civil powers
The work of the Army, Royal Navy and RAF EOD teams (bomb disposal) is always being called upon either in the form of giving instruction to British police forces (an arrangement made as a result of the Hoddington Report on the bombing of the Grand Hotel,

Brighton) or in coping with the occasional Second World War bombs that still turn up. A good recent example of this activity was when the sappers spent 46 hours at a Sheffield site working to dispose of a 1000kg Second World War Hermann bomb discovered during building excavation works, in the freezing February of 1985.

More sustained activity in the civilian realm is still carried out in Air/Sea Rescue by the RAF and the Royal Navy, whilst RAF Nimrod maritime patrol aircraft and RAF mountain rescue teams are on a permanent stand-by for search and rescue missions. The protection of offshore resources is another important sphere of activity, in the light of the increasing terrorist activity witnessed in the Eighties. Offshore oil installations make good targets. Offshore patrol vessels, Nimrods and the Commacchio Group of specially appointed Royal Marines, carry out continuous surveillance and defence exercises to make any such an attack a problem for terrorists with these targets in mind.

Future consolidation
A question mark hangs over the ability of the MOD, under the aegis of any colour of government, to sustain

Above: An RAF Sea King HAR Mark 3 Search and Rescue Helicopter lifting a stranded civilian to safety. A particularly good example of military forces in support of the civil powers. Many in the services welcome such opportunities to offset the considerable cost of purely defensive measures.

the improvements made to equipments without committing firm and substantial sums of money to do this. The Eighties until now has witnessed a thorough self-examination of the military body politic, the effects of which have by no means been fully felt. Some questions inevitably get asked that are almost too hard to take on board: for example, does the Army's Regimental structure enhance or impair BAOR's ability to train men effectively for the best possible type of Battle Group? Not many Army officials would relish changing such a traditional stronghold structure, even if it were deemed a necessity. But the main problem is as usual: funds. As civilian and regular MOD appointments disappear and as support, ordnance, medical, quality assurance and other traditionally Service establishments are pushed into the commercial civilian domain, there is a lot of pressure on all Services to substantiate and justify many of their roles and activities.

INDEX

A

PETER BANYARD was educated at Cambridge and has served with the British Armed Forces. He has since written extensively on militaray tactics and equipment both in books and a variety of military publications.

DUNCAN BREWER is a freelance journalist with a background in industrial relations, the new technologies and politics. He served with the RAF in Cyprus during the EOKA emergency and developed a special interest in the Falklands conflict.

CHRISTOPHER DOBSON is a war correspondant and author, winner of the IPC Award of International Journalist of the Year for his coverage of the Six Day War in Middle East and the Tet offensive in Vietnam. He currently lectures at the Police Staff College at Bramshill, and is the author a number of books on terrorism – but prefers fishing.

GILES EMERSON was educated at Oxford, and specialises in Science and Defence-related subjects on a full-time freelance basis. He worked for several years with the Central Office of information visiting a number of MOD establishments at home and overseas producing publicity and recruitment material.

MARTIN STREETLY is an aviation and electronic warfare historian who has contributed widely to various military and aviation publications, both as writer and technical illustrator.

Picture credits
All pictures and picture research for Forces '87 were provided by MARS Ltd of Stamford, Lincs. The Publisher would also like to thank the following organisations and individuals for allowing their photographs to be reproduced here:
Boeing, GL Bound, British Aerospace, Dassault-Breguet, MK Dartford, DOD, Imperial War Museum, Lockheed, MARS, MOD, National Army Museum, Royal Green Jacket Regiment, RAF, RAuxAF, Rex Features, Royal Navy, RNR, RNXS, Soldier magazine, Sikorsky, UKLF, USAF, US Army, US Navy, Westland helicopters.

Illustrations
Kim Church Associates
Richard Scollins
Paul Williams